Parables

Musings *from*
an Addict on *the*
Journey Toward
Wholeness

Jon Cerone

To my family and friends who always believed in me,
and to anyone out there who needs a little hope.

"You would be surprised to find that even the most beautiful flowers bloom in the darkest of valleys."

—E. Lomnicki (2013)

TABLE OF CONTENTS

AUTHOR'S NOTE

If you are here to change for the better, then come along for the ride.

However, whether you decide to read these musings will be up to you, but read it with an open heart and mind, nonetheless.

I do not claim to have the answers to your problems.

I only claim to have found some truth in my own struggles through life, addiction, and recovery.

There is no "correct" way to read this book.

I say that to make clear the idea that you, as the reader, are able to rearrange the chapters to better suit your plan of action.

If you wish to read them in the order that I have laid them out, you will see them from my point of view.

If you wish to start with the poem at the back or with the chapter on Discomfort, do so with the intention to alleviate whatever you are going through in these moments.

The readings are dense and reflective, but I do not intend for someone to read this book in one or two sittings. This book is for you to read in short spurts in order for you to reflect and put into action the insights you yourself have come across.

Whatever you have to do in order to take these lessons and use them for your own development.

Ultimately, wherever you are in your journey, I hope you find a way to utilize each of these chapters to best suit the needs of your lifestyle. I jump between them all to remind myself that the process is never linear or perfect! Life has a weird way of reminding us of its free nature, recurring lessons, and cycles. Don't be afraid to highlight phrases, fill Post-it Notes with quotes, scratch out words, rename chapters – whatever you need to do to get the most out of this book.

It's now up to you.

Part One

Prologue

There comes a moment in every person's life when they get tired of crying about the things they know they can change. We draw on these moments either to fuel our metamorphosis into a better person or to numb ourselves with pain to the idea of ever making any meaningful progress. I know this feeling all too well, thanks to my experiences with addiction, depression, and attempts at ending my life.

How many more nights, I often wondered, will I have to wake up in a pool of tears? How many more times will I shut out those who love and care for me because I am too afraid to meet their smiling faces? How many more days will I have to live with the shame of not having the confidence to change my life for the better? This dread will surely split me in two, and two again, until a million little fragments of me faded away into nothingness. And what will I have then? Nothing. A dream that never happened, a life barely lived.

Three years ago, in 2019, all those sleepless, tear-filled nights finally pushed me to the brink. I set out on a mission to free myself of my worst vices in order to take control of my well-being. I embraced my potential, reignited my motivation, and truly began to chase my dreams. The humbling experience of facing my fears and failures, coupled with the realization that I was capable of fixing my life, created the recipe for an introspective and fulfilling journey that I hope other people can learn from.

I tell you this with all sincerity: We are not perfect, but we also deserve to be reminded that we can make the necessary changes to live better lives – not just as individuals but collectively too. Believing in the words of others (such as me!) may be difficult, especially when we live during a time when people's opinions are as abundant as the thoughts in our minds. But I promise to be as authentic as possible with the insights I have gained through careful reflection and practice in pursuing personal transformation and aiding my fellow humans.

To say that I want to help others or, even more ambitiously, to help humanity remains an understatement. Before I could help others, I needed to learn how to help myself first. For what insights could I possibly offer if I was unable to bounce back from my own near death, spiritual as well as physical? How authentic would my words be if they were still draped with fresh denial and misery? Realizing the progress I have made – and continue to make – on my journey is what drives me forward with clarity. And with that clarity, I realized that my first task is to use my writing as a platform to remind you that the impossible is indeed possible; your dreams and aspirations are not out of reach; that it is not too late to turn things around for the better; that while the hand you were dealt in life may not have set you up to accomplish what you truly desire, there are more cards in the deck. Regardless of what you want from life or the extent to which you give meaning to the word "impossible," the opinions of others do not matter in the grand scheme of things. All that matters is you.

Finally, Honest

Without making this an autobiography, I want to share some points regarding where this writing originated from and the goals I wish to accomplish with this book.

I have been addicted to nicotine, marijuana, alcohol, cocaine, ecstasy, amphetamines, cough syrup, porn, social media, video games, television, sugar, and caffeine. For most of my adult life, I used all of these substances and activities to drown my inner conscience. Shame, failure, and the lack of self-forgiveness swirled within me as I battled the will to continue living.

Finally, after eight years of failure at recovery, education, basic human activities, and maintaining healthy relationships, I realized I needed to change or, more accurately, to take the process of change more seriously. My previous attempts at changing my life were doomed by a lack of planning and underestimating the depth of the bad habits I had fallen into. For the majority of those years of failing sobriety, recovering, and then failing again, I *always* intended to rid myself of all my worst vices and behaviors, but I always came up short.

My need for instant gratification destroyed whatever patience I had left, leaving me with an urge to fix everything at the moment. I would say, "This is it! This is the day

I change my life! All of these bad habits will be gone by tomorrow!" Not surprisingly, trying to deal with multiple bad habits all at once overloaded my psyche, and I would collapse right back into the whirlpool of substance abuse. Only after seeking *professional* help and being upfront and honest with my friends and family was I finally able to take the time and energy to make healthy moves in my life. I created a hierarchical replacement system to methodically organize my behaviors in a way to rid myself of dangerous addictions, vices, and habits while instilling healthier alternatives and activities along the way. As I've stated, I'm not here to give you a guaranteed, step-by-step process for fixing your life because everyone's interpretations and work ethics are different. My purpose is to offer questions, themes, and insights into possible thoughts and feelings that may cross your mind as you navigate your issues and journey.

Some people are addicted to sugar and unhealthy diets, while others are addicted to their smartphones, computers, and television screens. Some people are addicted to their jobs, careers, and hobbies, others to shopping, luxury items, and unachievable beauty standards. Some are addicted to violence, sexual desires, or stealing, and others to substances like alcohol, nicotine, and drugs. And it might be accurate to say that some people are addicted to hate – hate of health, happiness, love, and life.

We get addicted to things because we think immediate pleasures can fill the absence of love and happiness, the two essential qualities for a fulfilling, and healthy life. However, these "temporary" solutions become addictions and slowly but surely erode our intuition and sense of freedom. We might feel filled but rarely ever fulfilled. The less freedom we feel we have in our lives, the less genuine we feel, the angrier and more frustrated we become, and we begin to lash out at the world around us and the world within us.

This concept of *authenticity* can be best understood as a person's innate desire to choose their own way of life, which encompasses their physical, mental, and emotional well-being. The more things we get addicted to, the less freedom we have to choose how we want to spend our lives. Our autonomy is essentially handed over to the addiction. The resulting turmoil and consequences from the negative biases, mindsets, and self-absorbing habits that follow make it hard to identify who we really are under it all. The self–hate that develops swallows our will to live, leaving nothing but an empty shell.

I know this feeling too well, for I have been there multiple times. Only now, after years of tireless work and dedication, am I able to embrace my soul's full potential. After years of deliberate, consistent work, I am finally able to say, "I love myself for who I am and the life I am living." And if I still harbor regrets for the things I have done, I use every ounce of my being to learn from those mistakes and forgive my shortcomings. And while the results were few and far between when I began this journey, they started to add up over the weeks and months, and now people see a completely different person who is able to adjust and learn on the fly.

Expect Some Bumps

I don't want people to expect relentless positivity while reading this book. The journey through addiction toward healing and sobriety is hard work and all-encompassing. Some tough topics will be thrown into the mix because doubts, questions, and bad feelings are natural. We cannot run from the thoughts and tribulations our minds create in our darkest hours. We must face them. These inquiries are raw, and I want these words to reflect the reality we live in and to acknowledge some of the thoughts and feelings that may surface during our most depressing moments. If I were to leave out the insights I had from some of my darkest days, would this book truly encompass the requirements to understand what it will take to chase your dreams? After failing numerous times on my journey, the last thing I want is to give you something that doesn't prepare you to be the best version of yourself.

And it's okay to make mistakes along the way. You aren't the only one going through what you are going through. In addition to presenting the challenges, I also embrace hope. So read this book with an open mind and an open heart. What are you struggling with? How to chase your dreams? How to finally lose weight and take care of your health? Why do you rely on technology to make yourself feel real? Why do you feel your relationships are slipping away? Why do your thoughts always wander and why do you relentlessly find ways to distract yourself from what you really want?

We all have our own questions and reflections on our own beaten path. That is why we don't have to follow the same path to recovery or the same path to attain a desired state of well-being. I believe that everyone has the potential – the responsibility – to find out what that means for themselves. I cannot give you the perfect recipe for a better life, but I can give you hope that you'll be able to create your own. But now, more than ever, is the time to act.

Time to Act

With each year, humanity sinks further into a shell – a shell made of materialism, addiction, and shallow living. We rely on technology, media, the government, and religion to do the heavy lifting as we wade through life. Consider if any of the following sound familiar:

- "I'll just work for 45 years and finally retire like they want me to."

- "If something bad happens, the medical industry will save me, so I can treat my body however I want right now."

- "I'll get around to chasing my dreams and loving myself later. I've got all the time in the world."

Such thoughts are natural, and they span all ages. The saving grace is that we are never truly lost or so far gone that we can't turn things back around with a little hard work.

Human beings are remarkable creatures, and we need to remind ourselves how adaptable, compassionate, and tenacious we are. It took me seven years of trying to get sober to succeed finally. It took nine years to graduate from college. I am nearly 30 years old and still undoing the damage I selfishly did to my body, attitudes, and relationships. I am almost 30 years old and still finding new things about life that inspire me to soak up every moment. I keep reminding myself that it's still possible to heal and dream. It's possible to be healthy and happy. I am here to tell you that we can do it – that *you* can do it!

At first, I did not want to write about an "unfinished product": Me. Deep down, I knew I was still resisting some of the issues that were holding me back mentally and emotionally. I felt that whatever I wrote couldn't possibly help anyone because it would be tainted by my "failings." Do not misunderstand me, however. I'm not stating that a perfect me can be reached. Instead, if I am to write about shedding the skin of my old self, conquering of destructive habits and fears, and the fortitude to chase my dreams, it's important that I keep practicing what I preach. I am still in the process of taking my first step, for every day I am reminded that I need to be just as excited and ready as the day I set out on my recovery." My foot has not yet touched the ground; it's hovering there as I stand trembling in fear, wondering if I have the courage to walk this path, to become confident in my decisions. I have been at this crossroads before, and it left me scarred and hesitant.

This time, however, it will be different. As a rite of passage, I know what I must do. The final shackles of my primordial brain must be released, and I do so intentionally. I must become open to the world and confident with the positive outlook I have crafted for myself. The struggle to be a better you is ongoing: it happens every moment, every day, every year. People don't realize that the fruits of these efforts may take years to blossom fully. Those who succeed are the ones who embrace the small victories, so be realistic. Discouragement kills progress – even if you hit a wall because life is too much. But whatever you do, don't go backward. Slipping into old habits will undo your best and bring up the worst. At times like these, reflect on what you need to learn. Trust my words, the words of an addict. They are filled with experience and love.

Age is a state of mind. Energy is a state of the body. Wisdom is a state of the soul. Control over your mind allows you to perceive your age as only a number. Control over your body will enable you to use your energy as efficiently as possible. Having control over your soul will allow you to learn and humbly experience life to its fullest. Perception is truly the philosopher's stone—the grand elixir. How you look at things can turn any hell into heaven and garbage into gold. That is something I've learned from my journey over this last past decade.

My Journey

I've been writing since I was 14 – nearly fifteen years ago. I am, by no means, an expert on this topic, but based on hard-earned experience, I am confident enough to place my findings on center stage but with the same humility that got me here. I started writing poems, moving into short stories and philosophical musings until I formally studied philosophy at Grand Valley State University in Allendale, Michigan. Unfortunately, due to substance abuse, depression, and social anxiety, I was unable to finish my degree. This was a shock because formal education had come easy to me until college, and I fell into years of shame-ridden substance abuse. Looking back, the impacts of my addictions and failures should have either killed me or destroyed me to the point of being unable to keep living as a civilized human being, much less articulating my thoughts philosophically or in any kind of scholarly way. Fortunately, after years of attempting sobriety and finally taking the healing process seriously, I got a few sober years under my belt to set a sturdy foundation for a much brighter future. With a newfound appreciation for life, I finished my bachelor's degree in philosophy at the University of Illinois, Springfield. This accomplishment corresponded with a healthier lifestyle in terms of diet and exercise, but it was also accompanied by different perspectives on priorities, relationships, emotions, and goals.

Now, you may be asking the same question as my loved ones and peers after completing a degree in philosophy:

"What are you going to do with that?" To be honest, I usually reply with, "I don't know. Write a book?" More difficult to explain is that my study of philosophy allowed me to transform my emotional and chaotic thoughts into what I hope is a relatable and understandable narrative that I wish to share with you, the reader. But as I stated, I'm not too keen on writing an autobiography; putting my life on display in that manner is not appealing. I would rather be more creative by arranging my thoughts, insights, and experiences into short essays of reflections, revelations, and introspections. I want to share the highs and lows of my journey through addiction and sobriety to remind others that no matter your circumstances or the magnitude of what you want to achieve, you can reach your goals and realize your dreams.

Time To Begin Yours

The entries in this book encompass all the trials and tribulations that came with the territory of chasing my dreams and a healthier way of life. Your decision to start the journey, confusion on where to start, doubts about your ability to do it, the inevitable setbacks, the ongoing challenges of day-to-day living, and finally realizing that you might actually succeed are a few of the themes I present in the book. They are broken down into four phases that you may recognize, rearrange, or rename. However, you see fit. For me, "Visualize" was the first step in setting out on the journey of rebuilding myself because I needed the confidence and motivation to see the end product: my happy life. "Discomfort" deals with the doubts and raw feelings that overtook me during a time when the task of changing my life and lifestyle felt lonely and empty. "Perspective" is dedicated to exploring our perspective on matters that negatively impact our lives while reinforcing the need for positive beliefs that propel us forward. Finally, "Hope" will encourage you to succeed and persevere with reassuring essays on staying positive and grounded through-out your journey.

These essays and reflections may seem sporadic at first glance, but while similarities will be found throughout the different chapters, the theme for each chapter will ultimately stand out. The similarities reflect that no matter where you are in your story, rehab, or dream, you are still the same person deep down. You are just learning how to deal with yourself and your questions differently.

I understand that some of you may only skim through this material. Others will read it more thoroughly. No matter how much or how little time you take, I'm glad it's in your hands, and I hope you are blessed with a renewed perspective and motivation.

I sincerely wish that you find the courage, humility, and vigor to pursue your dreams and well-being. Even if you slip up and fall back into old ways, allow this book to find you during those dark times. And when you are finally at a place in your life where you are happy, healthy, and proud, you will share this book with those in your life who need a blessing and a boost. I hope the world finds new ways to love and communicate, for we are truly nothing if we don't learn to love ourselves.

It's now up to you. Do not be afraid to ask others for help, especially professionals or people in your life who have already conquered the same obstacles that are facing you.

Take the time to understand yourself, but that doesn't mean you have to do it alone. Become part of the world around you. And while it's scary to return to the place that crushed your dreams in the first place, this time you'll be ready. Because what we do with fear is what defines us. We can run from it, hide from it, poke our head out occasionally to be quickly reminded that it's still there before ducking back down. Or we can face it, using it as fuel to build a future self that will be more prepared to meet those same fears with greater aptitude.

How will you respond? Do you trust yourself enough to stay grounded, take the hit, and keep going? Or does it feel too big for you, too much to handle? I think not.

You are ready.

Brace yourself and start changing today!

Visualize

It's easy to let the world tell us what we are capable of and what we should be doing.

Majority of us are generally conditioned only to pursue matters that make acceptable amounts of money while our souls slowly deteriorate after every choice we make. And when we finally do take the time to pursue our deepest desires, we may fail at first and then get berated by a society that is supposed to encourage us instead of bringing us down. Our past follows us around like a shadow, reminding us of our so-called "inadequacies."

But these inadequacies are falsely labeled! Falling short of a goal should not be met with permanent shame. Rather, it should be met with imagination, reassurance, and optimism. But that's not something we teach much today. We let the biases and expectations of other people mold us into versions of ourselves we don't actually love. And once we are unable to love ourselves, we are unable to live life safely and happily.

Fortunately, we deserve to be happy, and we deserve to love ourselves. We deserve to know that we can make our dreams come true, no matter what they are. Don't let the haters fool you. Everyone has something they dream of doing, becoming, or attaining. Some people dream of ridding themselves of destructive addictions and habits. Some dream of finally taking their health seriously and getting into the best shape of their life. Others dream of starting their own business and using their ideas to bring smiles to the faces of their customers. Still, others wish to travel and see the beauty of planet Earth and the awe-inspiring sights of humanity's greatest cities. And some simply wish to find love and start a family, to give selflessly to those they care about. Even if these dreams seem typical, they are important for someone, and not everyone is blessed with the luck to attain them without effort.

If everything I just listed was easy to obtain, I believe the people of this planet would be in a much happier state than they are right now.

They are not.

Nevertheless, we must stay optimistic and tell ourselves that such goals are, in fact, our dreams, for it is easier to fight for a dream than something we label an "accomplishment." Either way, we must change ourselves to achieve them. We can't let others or failures from our past convince us that we aren't good enough. We have to *visualize* that we are capable of changing, that we can become the main characters of our own success stories, and overcome the obstacles we used to believe were insurmountable. We must tell ourselves it is time to change *now* before we forever lose the will to live genuinely. *Visualize* your potential and face your fears. No matter how long it takes, I promise you that the journey will be worth it in the end. All you have to do is be true to yourself and take the first step.

Standing in front of the mirror, I can see who I am now. I am a new version of myself that is in constant flux with how the world perceives me and how I perceive myself.

Trying to meet the expectations of others is a recipe for failure. The only visualization of myself I need is the one I hold dear, deep down inside me. This visualization does not require a mirror; a mirror only casts a reflection – nothing more than the opinions of others who have shaped me into what I do not want to be. Although some of those opinions were helpful, I must be fair and shed them all. It is time to open myself up to the idea that I am capable of changing, capable of becoming happy, healthy, and fulfilled without any outside props. I must be realistic in my approach but also filled with imagination to fuel my inner dreamer. I smile at the praise from friends, family, and peers and head toward new beginnings with vigor. I smile at the criticisms from others, myself, and my enemies, for I accept the challenge of proving them all wrong. Let me use this conscious mind to its fullest potential. Let me become whom I am destined to be.

The universe will bless you with enough money to survive life's trials and enough time to master your craft. All you need to do is start.

I know that may sound ridiculous, for I don't know the extent of people's financial struggles or time management skills. However, I can tell you that by putting your well-being first and following your heart to do what you love, you will ultimately find the correct time and money you need to aid you in your journey. "Correct" may seem like an ambiguous term for such a serious matter, but let us be intentionally vague for the moment and assume that it means enough money to pay the bills and secure resources to live (e.g., food and shelter), enough time to unwind in a healthy manner (e.g. take up hobbies or go on vacation), with enough left over to pursue your passions and dreams (e.g. more substantial goals). You may have to work a job you don't like, cut spending on things you enjoy, or change your diet to get your body and mind back to a desired level. Sounds exhausting, right? You might be thinking, "Is he crazy? This doesn't sound enjoyable at all! I just want to follow my dreams, not go on a diet or cut my spending or work at a job I detest."

And yet that's what it may take and likely what brought you to pick this book up in the first place. Like the need to engage in things we don't like the thought of in order to get to the things we want, this book does the same. No one ever said that living your best life would come easily; achieving your dreams takes hard work. That feeling of exhaustion I mentioned above may sound dreadful, but the rewards will be worth it. The journey of finally changing your life, of seeing and feeling the results, is incomparable to any other.

Moreover, my activities and routines aren't grandiose or divine answers to life's unsolvable mysteries. They just happen to plague the minds of the average person in the 21st century when left undone and unattended. Why do you want more money? Why do you want to be in better shape? Why do you want to stop using technology to fill the void in your soul? Why do you want to build more genuine relationships with others?

I will tell you why: Because you are a dreamer. Or, more simply, because you are human.

We just forget these things after letting the world beat us down for so long. I do not care how impossible you may think your dreams are to achieve. They are not; you are the only one who can make them happen. You want to be able to count on yourself when life gets difficult, right? You want your loved ones to count on you to be there, right? There is a version of yourself in your loved one's mind that sees you as the best version of yourself. There is also a version of your best self in your mind that you know you can achieve. So don't let your inhibitions get in the way. Don't let a couple of instances from your past plague your self-visualization and make you lose faith in your ability to achieve. You are capable of becoming the change that you visualize. You are capable of chasing and attaining your dreams. I may have to say that a million times for people to understand it to its fullest extent. And if they don't? I may have to find another way to say it a million more times!

You should be proud – even ecstatic – that you have figured out how capable you truly are. Embrace your new perspective and intuition. Entertain, enlighten, and educate yourself. We are all here for a purpose — it is grand to us, no matter how big or small it may seem to others.

It is pretty overwhelming to realize the importance of *visualization*: how we feel, sense, and interpret the world around us and inside us. For years, I let my addictions and bad habits ravage my self-perception and the health of my body and mind. The shame from failure and hate piled up until I could barely breathe, barely see. Desperate for a way out, I finally got tired of the tears I shed, the mask I wore, and the excuses I uttered. Through determination, discipline, and gratitude, I realized my purpose: to heal myself and share what I learned with others. Now I am here to say, "Until my last breath, I promise to use everything I have to help this dying world." I wish to help people understand themselves and the world around them, not from a scientific or political point of view but a psychological and philosophical one, with an emphasis on preventing the opinions of others from ruining your life.

The critic inside always tells us we are not meant to succeed and that we should just give up and choose a life filled with safety and comfort. Comfort only gets us so far, however. Years will pass, and we end up feeling empty inside.

By comparison, a dreamer's mind is dazzled with inspiration and energy. How to use this power is where we tend to fall short. Sometimes we don't know where to start or how to keep rolling once we take our first step. And once this happens, we often shut down and retreat to the safe corner we've made a home of. Sometimes you have to tell yourself, "If the world won't cut me a break, I will break my perception of the world instead." Start over! As long as you are alive, there isn't a single "absolute" that can keep you from changing and rearranging your perception of yourself and reality. Find a new angle and believe in yourself.

Don't get held up at the starting line because you fear what the critics will yell as you take your first step. Don't let these so-called hindrances or enemies of visualization get in the way. Just go and never look back. Be brave for your own sake and not for those who may themselves be fake. Be you. If they want to disapprove as you leave the beaten path, so be it. Be peaceful in your response. Be cool, calm, and collected. Stay centered. And above all, be happy and grateful.

In this age of "too much" information, we use technology as a way to make our lives easier. But this newfound efficiency comes with a cost because we end up signing over little pieces of our authenticity to make the rote experiences of everyday life – shopping, dining, chatting – more accessible. With this trade, we find ourselves alone. We may be in contact with the world digitally, but in reality, we feel stranded. You can watch only so many inspirational videos before you tell yourself, "I have no idea how to start being a better person." We won't find all of our answers by watching other people live. We have to experience the world directly through our sensations while drawing inspiration from those who have succeeded.

By no means am I downplaying the positivity and validity of some of what we find on the internet. I am merely saying that we need to use it differently. The infatuation we feel *watching* people live their best lives is our experience of vicariously believing that we can have that same success or feel those feelings. But there are few instruction manuals to help us apply the information we receive from the internet. Instead, we spend hours upon hours watching life happen, only to be left broken at the end of the day because we didn't use our time to make any real progress. We have to remind ourselves to put our phones down and turn our televisions off to free ourselves from their demands and make room for our inspiration. Unplug yourself, re-evaluate what needs to be done, then head toward it full force.

You may lose everything you hold dear because the universe is trying to remind you that you still have yourself.

You are not hopeless. You have the ability to visualize a better tomorrow.

Sure, life may feel full. You may be gaining new skills, new relationships, and new outlooks on life because you diligently put in the work and reap the benefits of the seeds you have planted. How you react to setbacks, enjoy small victories, or bring depth and honesty to your relationships are important. Still, these progressions are only analogous to the true magnitude of your journey. They are not in and of themselves the accumulation of knowledge, perseverance, and wisdom. Those particular checkpoints are internal to who you are – the uniqueness that is you, the reflections felt and seen through the expressions on your face, the power of your soul and presence mirrored through your eyes. You may be standing next to your fancy new car, but only the shallow will marvel at it instead of the glow you have cultivated from years of determination. So work hard and reward yourself but don't lose sight of your pure and simple essence. Being genuine in this way is often overlooked in a world where everyone wears a mask and is playing some part. So, smile big with the spirit you were born with.

Deep down, I have never doubted or feared my ability to be and stay creative or my ability to humbly accept that I needed help in adjusting my visualization of mental and physical well-being. At one point, though, I was terrified that my creativity, intuitions, and drive to be a better person were being dulled and replaced by my substance abuse and overuse of technology. Now that I am sober and in control of my devices, I can honestly say there is not a doubtful cell in my body or any part of my soul that feels I am running out of time to complete my dreams and ambitions. In fact, I am overwhelmed by how much I love all of my hobbies and healthy routines while struggling to find time to do them all. I am also excited about wanting to share my newfound enthusiasm with others so they can find solace and progression in their lives as well!

My life without substances was usually organized and well-planned, but I was not so structured during my abuse phase. Looking back, this unorganized attempt at living helps explain why I was unable to accomplish what I wanted to do. Before my addiction to drugs and technology, I used structure to help with schoolwork and my part-time job, and I lacked the structure to start writing poetry. During my addictive phase, I lost the ability to balance structure and creativity, trying to force one onto the other. You cannot put a schedule on creativity or motivation. You cannot decide when it comes and goes or when to work on this or work on that. You need to be flexible, so when those creative urges arrive, you'll be ready to create at the highest, most beautiful level. Life is too short to give up on the things you want to accomplish. Just remember that there is a time and a place for everything, and create a space in your life for all of it.

I want to save this world, so the ones who aren't here yet can experience the joys in life: the smiles, the smells, the sensations.

I am so excited to be alive that I can't bear the thought of not being able to feel like this! How boring would it be not to live? We take our time on this planet for granted and fill our life with numbing agents and bad habits. We owe it to the ones still to come and the ones who have passed to give true "personal change" the effort it deserves. The planet cannot handle our voracious consumerism forever. We can only blame each other for so long until we reach a point where we have to band together. But before we take that on, we may want to ask ourselves, "Am I ready?" And the answer is, Of course, you are! There are too many people to prove wrong to give up now.

I am certainly not the only one who wants to give people hope. We need more heroes for those who don't have the heart to follow their wildest dreams—heroes who remind people that they don't have to worry any longer. No matter how cliched, cheesy, or naive it may sound, I will be there for them. *We* will be there for them, show others that you need not be a slave to the nastiness in this world. You *can* master positivity, ingenuity, and authenticity. Shed the skin of your old self. Cast aside the cocoon that shielded you from the world so you can burst forth into beauty not seen before. Keep saying that you are ready, and it will get easier to get your body and life moving in the right direction. This relentless and outspoken series of personal reflections was written solely to help those finally ready to change their lives.

Another hindrance to visualization is forgetfulness. We forget how truly talented we are.

The mundane activities we do to survive dull the light that shines. Then, over time, we forget why we lost faith in our lives in a slow, steady process that buries the answers alongside the questions we used to ask so intently. We failed a couple of times and accepted what the world told us was true and right. We forget why we cry at night. We forget why we have to live a life that is actually a lie. The world that feeds us technology and media want to dim our fire. We mindlessly live for the quick buck, but is that an honest living? What is it to live honestly and authentically? Unhinged and unfiltered, with no need for a disposition from a celebrity or politician or fancy words and smiles from a New Age magician here to trick my people into an unconscious state of spiritual submission.

I do not claim a system or knowledge that is judgmental, vindictive or draped in a pretentious mission. You should be this, or you should be that. Such labels tell me where our species is at having no identity, so we condemn each other for having any opinion at all. And I don't claim to be a saint. We are all the same: Hypocrites too proud to admit that anything is wrong. Maybe our pride will be our undoing, but who knows? I am not psychic. I am just trying to figure out how to calm the world down a bit. Maybe that's my way of trying to calm myself down. Could it be that we are not so different after all? Or has the media done too good a job at dividing us?

I sincerely hope that even in old age, I will strive to be as selfless as possible.

Even if I'm facing a life-or-death situation, I can still fight for the freedom and understanding of my values and those held by others. I hope to be like my heroes, who have inspired me throughout the years to be tenacious and never give up on facing my fears and mistakes. I hope to share this knowledge and motivate others to do the same in their lives. As I write, I keep thinking to myself, "I hope . . ." as if there remains some uncertainty in the values of my future self. I only hope the mundane lifestyle of safe civilian living does not destroy my ambitious disposition. And yet again, I remind myself that if alcohol, drugs, depression, and suicide could not beat me, I sincerely doubt that something like that could either. I will keep practicing "heroism" and fine-tuning my commitment to becoming selfless. Without it, I feel an emptiness. I *hope* to be in the kind of situation that gives me opportunities to help people the best way I can, and for that, I must "put myself out there" for all the world to see.

Visualize this: Let us stay young at heart and find places of solace even as our jobs and this world try to tear us apart.

I have to keep reminding myself that the world will always find a way to give me a reason to doubt myself, which means I have to try even more challenges to pull that beautiful soul out to inspire those who have barricaded themselves behind armor and fake smiles – the way I used to do. I let a couple of people take advantage of my compassion; after that, I did not want to share my true self with anyone. Then, as time passed, I forgot how much I meant to people. I forgot that those nearest to me still believed in me and that others were waiting for me to help them on *their* journey.

There is no reason to hold back on who we truly are. If people look to take advantage of you, step up and protect yourself because they will not stop until you do. In fact, they will think they are in the right for doing so and make you feel worse for trying to stop them. All you can do is smile, for hating them for their inability to empathize is no better than their selfishness. We must be the more forgiving party. Forgiveness, however, is a difficult value to nurture, and the negative qualities of others often attach to us like parasites. Of course, surrounding ourselves with honorable people will help put us in a position to cultivate those positive qualities.

We have also forgotten what love is. Most people want nothing to do with love or compassion because you cannot make money off it. Shallow people will do whatever they can to put dollar signs on everything, and if you don't go along, if you stand your ground and try to be genuine, then you will be cast aside. Ignore them. You must stay strong and true. There is a good chance they will never understand, so don't hold it against yourself if you feel you could have helped them but didn't. It is not mean to think that some people will never change; it is, in fact, realistic. We give everyone the benefit of the doubt because we want to believe they have the potential for love, but they usually need to figure things out independently. You cannot save everyone, so focus on saving yourself first.

I will no longer hold onto my misunderstandings of other people. If they find the courage to change after meeting me, so be it. If they continue to walk on the path of selfish pride, then so be it. I am only here to offer the tools necessary for self-reflection, change, and self-love. If, by sharing these tools, I find myself at war with those who seek to take advantage of this world for selfish gain, then so be it. I am done pitying those who knowingly shy away from bettering themselves, and I will not regret this. It is not my job – or yours – to save everyone; even if it was, not everyone could be saved. Words are so fragile and fleeting, and there is no way to know if your lessons and advice will reach the hearts and minds of those who struggle. All you can do is lead by example, live your best life, and hope for the best for everyone else. Lend a helping hand when you can, and cheer humanity on as we undo the damage of narcissism and materialism. The undying commitment to make the world a better place will never die. My heart overflows for those of you who still have hope and have decided to turn away from media, money, and ignorance. For you, there will always be a way forward.

My visualization becomes clearer the more often I fail.

Instead of dwelling on mistakes, I now use them to propel me toward something unexplainable. My will and drive are untamable. The less I try to restrain myself, the happier I become. I am coming out of my shell. This time it is different. All the previous times I spoke of my goals and prowess, I used drugs and pride to reassure myself that "I still got it," knowing it was a ruse to cover my doubt that I still had a chance to bounce back. It was not a path to discovering my most authentic self. Now, however, I feel wings beginning to unfold from my back. Every day that I beat addiction, I grow another feather.

I used to take my anger out on the human race for casting me out and making me feel like a heathen. I did so by cynically thinking that the world was against me without actually doing anything to confirm this belief. I preferred to wallow in my victimhood because I would rather be lonely. Shovel enough drugs, sugar, technology, media, and propaganda down your throat, and you will know the feeling of being truly evil, of wanting life – including your own life – to perish. The fact that I bounced back from this abyss is nothing short of a miracle I finally made because I could no longer live the other way. But this change was not just *my* doing. I share the credit with friends, family, and peers who supported and helped me along the way. Still, I had to take the first step. I had to want it every moment of every day. Now I have it and will do everything I can physically, emotionally, and mentally to secure this feeling for the rest of my days.

My progress from hopeless addict to the epitome of health and determination is driven by my innate nature to evolve and adapt but in a way that lets my true self grow, unafraid to be known. I am the embodiment of karma – the good and the bad, the cause and effect. I am content with knowing nothing. I welcome the opportunity to battle any trial that life sends my way. My greatest feature is an inability to give up or go down without swinging. I have fallen further than almost everyone I know, and I have only grown stronger from everything and everyone that tried to deal me a lethal blow. My confidence has returned, something I became unfamiliar with due to my failures and the judgmental asides of others – who, I might add, are far from perfect themselves. I finally have a life I can be proud of, something I can show to those who didn't believe in me, tried to make me like everyone else, and sought to impose their limited values, making me doubt myself.

Now it's time for revenge, but nothing malicious, of course, or even at the level of, "I told you so." My revenge is the eradication in my mind of "doubt,' and I will accomplish this by living a happy, healthy life. I do not require intimacy, religion, drugs, society, media, or government to feel the way I do. I am the independent variable, the hero in my own story. A man who finally crafted himself not for glory but to see others catch fire as he did. A warrior committed to cleansing this planet of ignorance and planting new seeds of compassion and understanding. The forces of nature swirl around me, caress me and nurture me. I am the force that rectifies the subjective and condemns the objective, illuminated by the beacon atop my head. The galaxy opens up to me. The only way my journey was possible was from sheer determination to rid my mind and soul of the judgments and restraints placed on me by my misunderstandings. I can finally let go. I hope you feel as though you have written this yourself, for only through my encounters with others was I capable of understanding that we all hold the same potential.

This is the story of a man who risked everything to be a little more unique and authentic than the world expected him to be. To seek rebirth, like nature, with roots shooting through whom he used to be in order to connect him to who he has always been, awakening to the enlightened side of life that most would consider "taboo" – too dangerous or difficult to contemplate. But what is taboo to someone who searches for truth?

Allow me to reminisce. No one expected this fellow to bounce back. Everyone thought he was done for, that there was no way he could make anything out of the life he took for granted and then soiled. Their grave mistake was that they neglected to dig deeper to find the seed he left in the soil years ago. Although left unwatered, it still lived and breathed, waiting for the moment to take root and sprout up to touch the sky and shade those who always believed in him. "I will protect you," he said.

He doesn't worry that others scoff at his dream. If this life forgives him for his most heinous deeds, why can he not reciprocate that to others? To waste time worrying about consequences impedes his ability to live and act in the moment. He realized that only by being straightforward and honest would he be able to nurture the pure nature of himself. The greatest evil – and in turn, the greatest regret – is defining oneself by the expectations put in place by others. What are you doing if you aren't chasing and living your dream? You aren't living. You are just waiting to die. Slowly.

Nature breathes with us, but concrete suffocates, making us lose sight of what is important: The fact that we are alive! We get so wrapped up in what the world is doing that we forget what *we* want to do. This world crushes dreams, but it does so in a way that makes people okay with it by letting them know they are part of the same group, so no one thinks less of themselves because, in the end, we all give up anyway. Our ideals became frail after allowing the world's opinions to shape our minds – opinions that become beliefs that society embeds like cement in our psychological foundation that takes years to chisel away. And there are some who will never find the pickaxe to get started. But what may seem like a dead end may actually be the beginning of another route. So keep moving, for heaven's sake, so may we find another way.

I transcend yet again.

This time, I intend to escape the last shackle finally. Up until now, I was afraid of the unknown. It terrified me because I was worried about what I would think about after I healed. I have mostly known only pain and manic frenzy thanks to unhealthy coping mechanisms and deep-rooted unforgiveness. The unknown beckons me now, however. The nothingness of the future invites me, and I wait at the moment for its presence to engulf me. Now that my will has become positive, I can make a break for infinity it it all falls together while I start falling upward. Isn't it beautiful? Who knew that the mind of a sober drug addict could legitimately reach for the stars? This calls for a toast! To love and the pursuit of knowledge. Let each of us aid our fellow man and finally become one with what has always existed, always listened, always whispered. The voices of peace, tranquility, and revelation carry me to a new reality, yet it feels like I have been here before – or have I been here all along? Ahh, the endlessness of it all! Persistent is the nature of this reality, this innocence. I have only just begun to refract light through the prism of my mind. Clear as clear would a mind be if it could finally see what it needed to be and be open to all possibilities.

Discomfort

Visualizing your potential and your desire to be true to your dreams is just the first step in achieving them. You must first visualize what you are capable of before giving your utmost attention to such a journey. Of course, it is easier to dream and to visualize success and luxury. We do it all the time. Where we fall short is the next step, which involves changing our habits to set ourselves up for working efficiently, gratefully, and consistently.

This phase of the journey is called *Discomfort*, as it marks the period where we come to grips with the realization that some of our comfort zones must be cast aside in order to change and grow. The future self we seek is only obtainable by our conviction to make difficult changes in our lives.

Be warned that the foundation we build during this phase may be painful, real, and unsettling, but these steps are necessary to craft a new perspective of the world and ourselves. There may be some activities, substances, and people in our lives that are not the best influence in terms of helping us construct good habits. We may need to say goodbye to them to recollect ourselves and gain a sense of clarity.

This phase is not forever, however. The people who understand the severity of your situation will be patient as you take the time to be a better person. You will also attract new people into your life who reflect your changing values. Those who demand that you stay in an unproductive rut for selfish reasons will have to be dealt with accordingly, and it may not be easy.

We must face this discomfort and calmly keep heading towards a better understanding of (and commitment to) our true intentions. During that process, we may wonder, "Why am I lonely? Will this be worth it? Why do I hate myself? Will I ever be good enough?"

These discomforting questions may be loud at first, but this is only because we have buried them deep below our pain and coping mechanisms. We need to ask them, though, no matter how deafening the sound, and then face the answers with tenacity.

Am I good enough? Am I strong enough to muster the courage to do this? Will these tears ever stop?

I have become exceptional at questioning everything – even the most basic concept of self – and have become confused with no direction, no answers, no definition, and not a single absolute to build off. It's just me, floating end-lessly with no conviction. Other people's ideas swirl around me and through me, slowly and heavily. I am waiting for the universe to kick me into gear so I can finally do what I have always dreamt of doing: being the person I dream of being. I keep saying hopefully to myself, "I will *eventually* get around to that whole, sober, happy, healthy life and deal with those traumas." But deep down, I know it feels impossible. Maybe I can pretend that I am trying my hardest and then give up and leave town so I don't have to face my loved ones. Depression is a good excuse. Hell, I might as well be dead inside. Such laziness. But not taking the time to understand why I am sad or how to combat the consequences of my actions is what real laziness looks like.

I am giving you the ultimatum to release your worst vices or risk suffering for the rest of your days with constant thoughts of inadequacy and shame. You will detest everything about yourself, your choices, and everyone around you. You will continue to wallow and barely make ends meet for no other purpose than to seek instant gratification through different routes of stimuli and numbing agents. There is no balance when using these substances and activities. No matter where you go or look, this world will flood you with temptations to spend money destroying your mind and body, all for temporary pleasure and short-lived experiences. Everyone needs a release; hell, everyone needs a vacation. But can you say that your options include working out, reading, writing, meditating, painting, singing, dancing, being grateful, or anything healthy and positive? Is your life so hopeless that you choose to lose yourself in highly addictive and destructive behaviors?

Have you forgotten how to relax and enjoy your own company genuinely? When life and all its consequences pile up, do you freak out and immediately succumb to a safe place? That "safe place" is where your pain and lack of motivation infect you.

Remember: Every day is an opportunity to heal yourself. It may seem more convenient and familiar to destroy your body and mind, but deep down, you know what has to be done, even if the work requires you to be miserable for a while.

If I keep telling myself "Later," then "Now" will never come. Assuming "the future me" will work hard enough to make up for "my past self's" lack of motivation and direction is nothing more than the noise of an inflated ego draped in procrastination.

You can always say that you will be better tomorrow, that you will make the sacrifice, and start the journey when the timing is "right." In the meantime, today is an ode to the person you were, and as a parting gift, you decide to embrace your bad habits one last time. And again, you will say, "Tomorrow is the day." But tomorrow never comes if you keep living in the past, paying respects to a past "you" with no intention of becoming the strong, determined version of "you" that needs to start *now* to make all the next tomorrows worth living. *Today* needs to happen. Tomorrow cannot wait for the real you, and yesterday will eventually praise the work you do…. today!

Why is addiction such a weird subject?

Today we herald people who are addicted to work or their craft because we put money and accomplishments on some type of pedestal whatever the cost to get there. But when addiction is referred to in terms of drugs and substances, most people get cold feet knowing how to approach the subject properly. Even speaking about our addiction to sugar and fast-food is frowned upon because no one wants to be called unhealthy or overweight. No one wants to be reminded of their addictions because no one wants to be held responsible for their habits and behaviors. Addiction is a weird subject because the core concept of addiction is essentially about humans replacing the idea of an instant suicide with the process of a slow, degenerating, constant level of self-inflicted decline coupled with pleasure and fun. The momentary need of wanting to die is neutralized by the momentary want of pleasure – a dangerous combination.

We view such addicts as "lost causes". Instead of looking for ways to heal those who have fallen, we pity and shun them and hand them a businessman's tie. "Good luck with all that. Here's some change for your troubles." Maybe addicts aren't given enough credit because the nature of addiction comes at the expense of healthy relationships, financial stability, and overall health. And yet is it not worth noting that to keep living in the shadow of death and suicide *on a daily basis* might suggest the potential for transformation? That there is resiliency and tenacity at play that can be harnessed for positive outcomes? Maybe there is something to learn from addicts instead of acting like they are less than human. But I digress. The rock bottom feels safe. There is no more "down." I can finally rid myself of self-delusions and start fresh. It was time actually to practice what I preach. And if I did this soberly, I could finally live without expectations and attain mental, physical, and spiritual wealth. Maybe I could be resilient one day. Perhaps I should start learning today...

Here is another discomforting idea: You can run from your destiny to please your loved ones or a society that claims it knows what is best for you, but you will only be miserable in the end.

Destiny calls to you every day in mysterious ways, but we use substances and other distractions to ignore our souls and drown out the noise of our subconscious self. "This world is so loud, and I don't have the patience to calm myself down!" But if you reach for the TV remote or your cell phone, you will find the solace you are looking for . . . right? "Oops, tonight is lost. I will find the time to be better tomorrow." But still, there is something nagging us from the inside. A discomfort. A call. It beckons me, but I run, reaching for anything to still that voice, because by stripping myself of these comfort zones, I might end up barren, frantic, and empty. What will I fill myself up with then? Vegetables, a long run, a good book? Could they actually satiate the crazy being I have become? Am I ignoring the obvious by casting doubt on these healthy methods?

The reality is that they may initially miss the mark in occupying my manic need for something to feel in this moment, but my brain would not be offering these activities if I did not believe – deep down – that they will aid in my recovery. Recovery from what, though? Oh, right, my deliberate disregard for being a human being who needs balance and health. How could I forget? Maybe it's the fact that each day I feel like a lazy slug who is hopelessly crawling from one wall to another inside of my existence? Perhaps I should go for a walk and some fresh air? The television will be there when I get back.

It will never be enough.

I don't believe my efforts will ever be enough to warrant praise and recognition from my fellow humans. No matter how hard I work, the world will always want more from me. Therefore, would it not be better to simply live for me at my own pace? Is it not enlightening to realize that I will never be enough? My path does not require tireless effort for monetary gain or status. I work solely for the most integral part of my soul, which is drawn to aiding and entertaining others and creatively deciphering the metaphysical aspects of reality.

Sadly, it has taken me awhile to get here. I have been trapped in the hamster-wheel hierarchy of mindless peons who are spoon fed a standard living wage with social security and acceptance on the side. I have run myself ragged in hopes that my efforts may inspire me to work even harder. I have exploited my being in service to mundane activities to secure resources for survival while desperately seeking free time to work on my dreams and aspirations. I am exhausted, but as I said, "It will never be enough." But then to say, "I need a break," would be dodging the issue. My challenge is not a lack of rest; it is my perspective, the belief that I must work so hard, which causes my lack of rest. I don't want to live for anyone's sake but my own. I want to live, love, and rest at my own pace. I want a flow of life that works with me, not against me. It's time to pull back and formulate a plan of action.

I am tired of things that skew and misconstrue my idea of what love is.

I have done my absolute best to shed the behaviors and mannerisms that society has attempted to embed in me, but the screens keep pumping me full of them yet again. I do not wish to turn to hate, blame, and misunderstanding as quickly as this world has conditioned us to do. But to be calm in a swirl of such relentless stimuli is to be a ship being tossed in the middle of a terrible storm.

Maybe I'm overreacting and people aren't really worried about how we are all slipping into a desensitized stasis. Maybe it's just my town or my city. Is it true about my state, my country, my world? Maybe it is different on other planets or in other galaxies. Maybe somewhere they have figured out a more efficient and productive process for protecting the sanctity of species and planetary health? I sincerely hope so. But we cannot get ahead of ourselves and wish for a utopia. There must always be duality, polarity, the pendulum swinging between love and hate. It's tough to feel as though the scale is tipped in favor of the negative, but the signs do seem to lead us to this assumption. But maybe that's dependent on where I am looking? Must I search elsewhere? Do I need a break from modern living? Would I have to abandon my duty to this species if I resolved to only focus on bettering myself and my creative endeavors? Where is the balance? Where is the tranquility?

The only objective thing about pain is the fact that we all feel it. Otherwise, the intensity is subjective.

We try our hardest to relate to one another, but rarely do you meet people who put themselves in another's shoes. And that is precisely what this world is missing. Most of us have groups in which we connect and have a mutual understanding, but what about those outside of our friends and family? Why is it that as a species we are so distant from each other? Is it technology? Society? Ancient programming? Nature? We are all dying inside to be "one people," yet we live as though it is us against the world or us against the opposition.

Are we destined to destroy ourselves, or can we turn things around and save this dying planet? Do we all think these things, or am I the only one drowning in misery? Will I be silenced for making these thoughts public? Or will I sit here isolated, submissive, and intimidated by the media's power to spread bias and negativity? Why do I cry at night and feel like I don't belong? Why do I want to leave this prison of flesh? When will I use the gifts I've been given to make the world a better place? Is life really as dreadful as I make it out to be, or am I missing a key piece? What is peace? What is love? What is tranquility? Can we set aside our differences to solve the problems at hand, or will we nuke each other into dust at the end? If history repeats itself, does that mean there is no independent variable that could change the norm of despair? Can we change ourselves for the better so we can make the world smile again? I wish I didn't ask such redundant questions, but then what is living if you aren't willing to truly think.

What more could I possibly ask of myself?

It is bad enough how guilty I make myself feel for not living up to other people's expectations. But then to think I must deprive myself of life's simple pleasures – an ice cream cone, a funny TV show – because they might diminish my enthusiasm for being productive and pursuing my aspirations is madness. I guess because the universe stopped punishing me, I felt someone had to step in. No one would judge me or accuse me of pride or sloth if I did what was required to be "average." But my habit of being too hard on myself for not doing "enough" keeps rearing its ugly head, and I am left slamming myself into the ground like a railroad spike. I keep thinking that if I work myself hard enough, I will find a way to finally relax and ride away from this job, this city, this toxic pond. But I now realize this punishment is no longer necessary, for only by forgiving my sins and shortcomings will I finally be able to articulate my transcendence for the masses. It's exhausting, though. The back and forth between money, job, life, survival, and the world. When will it all become silent for me? When will the snow blanket my mind so I can sleep with peace? Or am I doomed to toil with an ever-rushing river of countless thoughts? I wish it was as easy as how my heroes make it out to be. I wish I had the courage to relax. I wish I had the courage to feel refreshed. But wishes get us nowhere, and this hopeless chump is still searching for a reason to live out his dreams instead of returning to dreary safety as a civilian cog in the modern machine.

I get so overwhelmed thinking of all the things I have to do and want to accomplish that I wear myself out to the point where I want to drift away to play video games or watch TV.

I am never invigorated enough to work on the positive, creative outlets I've lined up because I'm exhausted from thinking about them all day while also working a job. Thinking is work, and I think too much instead of doing. That is why I need a daily routine of meditation: to help mitigate the energy I dispel on overthinking, to teach me how to come to terms with my overthinking, and to better utilize my energy in a healthy, creative, positive manner. I don't need a particular way to do it such as someone else's plan or the traditional approach – just a simple way to calm my mind for at least ten minutes.

Regardless of what people tell you, meditation comes in many forms. It's not the practice of "no-thought," for example, for there is no such thing as stopping the thoughts within your mind. All you can do is let them pass, catch the ones that are beautiful, and continue on with the flow of time. The problem is that in this day and age, there are so many things distracting us from becoming calm. At every instance, something is trying to grab our attention. The overstimulation has made us drunk on information. I wish I did not have to join the digital world, but how else will I get myself out there for the people that need me?

I always get stuck in a rut when I feel like I failed because I didn't trust my own judgment or knowingly walked into a situation that was unwinnable.

I know I'm not perfect, and everyone makes mistakes, but sometimes I feel like I've failed someone, that I could not save them. But then why did this world send them to me? What was I supposed to learn from them? I have to realize, though, that it's not my job to save people; some people just want to be miserable, and it's a waste of time and effort to show them anything different – especially when I struggle myself trying to stay positive. Maybe we share that same struggle.

It makes sense that fewer and fewer people want to talk about their shortcomings in terms of their habits or mental well-being because they can no longer handle criticism. Instead, we look to social media to learn why others' lives are so interesting and worthwhile, yet we cannot translate that into our own understanding and application. So why allow myself to be swayed by the opinions and mannerisms of others? It's no wonder that addictive tendencies find a way to infiltrate even the most stalwart dispositions. The need to be like everyone else, accepted by everyone else, respected by everyone else, and related to by everyone else, is a recipe for failure. You cannot save anyone when you forget about your own visualization of yourself. Stop running from the conversation within your soul that requires you to face who you really are.

Recognizing that we may have addictive personalities is discomforting.

One thing I'm always wary of is that because I'm prone to becoming easily bored and possess such a high tolerance for pleasure, I can get so addicted to substances or activities that I ruin whatever pleasure they initially gave me.

I feel that even if I get addicted to the *positive* parts of life that I might end up hating them in the end as well. I am unable to use a throttle or to "moderate," which then makes me hate myself for not having self-control. My experience of life is so demanding and rewarding simultaneously that it's nearly impossible for me to ever slow down.

This is why I crumble, crash, and burn. I underestimate the potency of my feelings and let my impulses lead me with no regard for outcomes. This tendency has its strengths, as all things do, but I have yet to understand how to manage the consequences of this double-edged sword. The truly frightening aspect is how it affects all of my experiences. This unchained vigor catalyzes my addictions during times of substance abuse and is also responsible for my clinging to social media and technology.

Rechanneling that energy into activities and behaviors that are creative and rewarding will be my main task, but how many more life-altering challenges can I endure? Do I not realize that I am emotionally and mentally exhausted? Will it ever be enough to just exist? Or have I become addicted to self-improvement? Change is a burden that has us trying to heal and find peace in a frenzy of aspirations and distractions.

So, I stay humble and grateful that I have the opportunity to continue growing.

I used to proclaim things like, "It isn't fair. Some of these thoughts are heavy, and I don't know how to share them."

Unable to open up to anyone at the risk of being called crazy again. I cannot see the look on their faces – again. That worrisome pity they took on me. I have to step up, find the remedy, and balance this equation we call life. Find that fire and spark a revolution. Raise a fist and keep moving until I die. I cannot go back to the person I was or succumb to the same vices that brought all my misery and anguish. Even the trap constructed by the many screens, fiends, and data streams won't keep me tethered to my complacency.

As much discomfort I am feeling at this very moment, nothing will ever compare to the pits of addiction. I must find a way out of this unhealthy cycle of scrolling, stagnation, and unhealthy satiation. This phone seems surgically attached to my being and its many pictures and sounds spiral outwards toward my face. I throw it across the room in hopes that it destroys my televisions as well. But as I regain my senses, I realize that I am capable of this change. Maybe these thoughts aren't so crazy after all, and I might be the crazy one for not sharing them.

I am tired of the evil that snakes out from my back like tendrils.

Shrieking. Screaming. Menacing. Whispering about the destruction of the world, both around me and within me. When I succumb to my vices and then cry, I blame the evil side of my life, that eerie fire behind my eyes. Always wishing for the perfect use of my time, I end up wasting another day working for a useless dollar—a cog in the system.

Come back home and then polish off a bottle of Waddle on the way to the bathroom to vomit. Wake up in a rage as spikes raise up from the back of my head and my eyes gleam. Please devour the soul of this poor young man who can't catch a break. Tell him to listen to me, that by the end of the day he will be safely in the arms of the unforgiven. Shackles rattle and scrape as he tries to get comfortable holding nothing but the air in the corner of the room. The screaming gets louder. The spikes and tendrils rip through his flesh. This poor planet might cave inward as the darkness above sinks its roots deep into the soil. This hate is infectious. Deadly. Finally, he begins to breathe again. Slowly. Faintly. He regains his composure. The power to destroy isn't useless; it is simply misplaced. To let it run its course would be foolish, but to learn its ways and make it his own, well, that might be the only option left.

Perspective

As the scene finally calms down, the dust begins to settle just enough for us to finally see.

The chaotic metamorphosis has finally reached a silent crossroads. Is this the feeling of reassurance? What exactly are we reassuring ourselves of? That we have made the correct choices and are now tasked with understanding our short-comings and negative perspectives? A sigh of relief awaits us, for now our story unfolds more naturally. Our weaknesses are, in fact, the reasons that drive us to be better people. After coming to terms with the things we had to change and the perspectives that drove them, we now confront the mental aspect of our turmoil. Perspective is an amorphous notion with themes that range from time, relationships, depression, and shame to forgiveness and well-being.

We come to realize that we aren't perfect, which is the greatest blessing we could receive. We face our greatest fears with the same answers we used to run from. We come to realize and understand why we thought the way we did, and why we started on this journey in the first place. Imperfec-tions are the birthplace of inspiration. Whether it's to rid ourselves of deformities or find ways to mask them, this is the starting point and when we begin to grow. We may not realize it, but our greatest imperfections never go away. We learn to live with them to the point where we become pure, unchained beauty.

I am not perfect, and I have never claimed to be.

I have only hoped that my shortcomings did not come at the expense of other people's love for me. I still hang my head as if I haven't already suffered enough, punishing myself for thoughts and actions that have already passed. This is not the way of a hero or a person seeking to become one. This is the path of a broken, selfish soldier who wants to play victim. This hand will cramp with uncontrollable pain before I let baseless doubts hinder my work. To face my past with written words is to do the world a favor by showing people it's okay to dream and fail. It's okay to lose the love you once had. Just make sure you never give up, for if you do, your doubts and paranoia will win, leaving a shell of a soul to pick up the pieces.

There is no easy, step-by-step process for fixing your life or following your dreams. All I can offer you is a different perspective for tackling the changing landscape of motivation and determination in a world that evolves with technology. Maybe you'll find solace in the relatability of my words. Perhaps some truth, or potential, or the aesthetics. Whatever you find, do so with the realization that I don't claim to be right. I only share these thoughts with the intent of supporting your own personal journey. Maybe you can become your own hero? Perhaps you don't need my words? Perhaps we can spur change together? Find a reason to credit yourself for working hard, and the fruits of your labor will surely satisfy your desires.

I no longer wish to be overwhelmed.

The sheer magnitude of my creativity has had no throttle while existing inside me for the last seven years. I tried everything to calm the storm, but all my methods, from drugs to video games, were "inorganic" – they came from outside myself. Instead of learning how to flow with my natural impulses, I spent years fighting against them. A few people's opinions of some of my work sent me into a state of reclusion. I no longer wanted to share my writing, certain that people would tell me I'm crazy and ask if I'm sober. I shunned myself and made terrible excuses for why I no longer write. How many more conditions must I meet before "they" deem my psyche acceptable to society? Perhaps never, and I just need to find a way to articulate myself in a way that goes beyond frustration, hate, and despair.

Things are different now. This time they will have to listen. The refinement of my character will allow all of my selves to blossom together. People will be more inclined to listen to crazy if it's done calmly. I just have to go about it in a balanced way, finding moments of insight that flicker with enough passion to shed light on the questions we have left unanswered. The scale may only tip momentarily to allow the full utilization of a raw emission. Whether it's good or evil, too much of anything can upset the equilibrium. A conscious effort to reside in the now, the in-between, must be made to overcome the polarization that has infiltrated all aspects of our lives. For only by understanding *unity* may we fully grasp our ability to guide ourselves. And yet even my own overwhelming, hyperactive imagination stands next to my insensitive, logical, and realist nature. The throttle that regulates my attention was broken by never-ending substance abuse. Psychosis is deadly. Sobriety is heavenly. Patience is humbling.

Becoming more attuned to what the universe and your higher self are trying to tell you is a struggle. Practice makes perfect, though, and the result so far for me is worth more than all the riches in the world. What is better than truly, wholeheartedly being the most authentic you? I may not even know when I get there, but it won't matter as I will keep trying to be the best me, losing all biases and regrets in the process. I will learn to face everything head-on with a clear mind, an open heart, and a vibrant soul even in the face of adversity, heartbreak, or failure. I will not bend, wither, nor become susceptible to demoralizing habits. I will chase my dreams, laugh, love, and live to the utmost. I will pull up those around me and lend a hand to those who aren't ready to stand up on their own. Do not fear or fight your demons; befriend them. Do not worship or idolize your angels; respect them.

It seems unnecessary to keep writing the same things without taking the time to understand why I feel the way I do.

It is even more confusing because memories and the emotions connected to them that I thought were long gone resurface with the intent to break me down. Or build me up? I guess it's whatever I choose to do with them, yet that is the hardest part. There is always something to be grateful for, and there is always something to be sad about. That is life. Whether you choose to be great or worthless is up to you. For the first time in my life, I have the opportunity to happen – to *be* – with no restrictions. Thanks to my daily victory over addiction, there are no curtains, lies, masks, or biases. At long last, I am able to breathe easily. By accepting the chains of my past, I can own and resolve my pain with conviction. Cast aside the erroneous judgment that the world is at fault for plaguing your mind. Find the time and determination to be your most authentic self without using man-made institutions and their "reformations."

Reaching the goal of living a healthy, happy life does not begin by no longer doing the things you believe are holding you back.

It's about doing the things that propel you forward. In that process, you will slowly but surely find the feeling and motivation to cast aside the vices that hinder you. For if your mind is afflicted with the negative thought of "stopping," your intuition and soul will focus only on that. But let's say you change your perception to "start": start going to the gym, start eating healthy, start reading, start finding new healthy hobbies, and start keeping track of your screen time. When you focus on stopping a bad habit, that habit then enters your mind, and you find yourself succumbing to it. But when you switch perspectives, you have the power to start something better, something positive and healthy. So start today, and soon you will notice that you have finally stopped doing what you hated.

People change, perspectives change. No matter who you are or what you do, you will grow up to have problems.

In trying to reach some unrealistic goal of perfection, we will always fall short. The perfection we seek is on every screen. The media has mastered the act of convincing us that we're not good enough or that we need to buy or subscribe to something to fix ourselves or to experience something that is considered a must-do activity. It may be hypocritical of me to say this because I am part of that media with this book – I wish I could give it for free – but I am also a victim of this manipulative, money-driven world. And yet my intention for you is the opposite: to *not* feel inadequate on a daily basis. I want to give you the courage to rid yourself of those demeaning outlets so you can create new pathways for building yourself up. I write this for you as well as me so we can make peace with our imperfections and live life to the fullest.

Even though we bleed the same blood and cry the same tears, it seems that we, as a specie, have fallen away from the idea that we all want the same thing – to love and be loved, to be safe and live peaceably – and that even the plants, animals, rivers, and mountains are a part of us.

We are all life, happening together. Religion, politics, and technology want to strip us away from this idea of togetherness. Our vices numb us to our soul's lust to find a way to become one with life. I do not write or speak these thoughts with the intention of claiming to be right or be better than someone else. I ask only to follow me and I will show you a way to freedom. I will show you love. If we are to save this dying world from our ignorance, we must come together. The only things we should worship are our abilities to forgive and to grow. Only through this will we find the courage to change and to protect.

I came to these thoughts through my experiences with the people around me. They are responsible for these breakthroughs. So, find the real you. If I show you how to lend a helping hand, do the same for another. The world craves more forgiveness and compassion.

There is only so much of your past you can face before you are emotionally drained.

We must sometimes step back from being hung up on healing and working in order to relax and recharge and use what energy we have left to be happier and healthier. It is pointless to make yourself face your demons when you are exhausted, because facing an obstacle when you aren't prepared is a sure-fire way to fail. Only when we have prepared ourselves and our methods can we learn from our past and from life. I speak from experience when I say that all my efforts to free myself of my vices, whether it be alcohol, cocaine, pornography, television, sugar, sex, my cell phone, or nicotine, fell short when I did not take the severity of my situation seriously. I find that I am more susceptible to crass desires when I am not well-rested and prepared. By "prepared" I mean that I had no new outlets to replace the vices I was fighting. It was also foolish of me to try and muster the motivation or do the legwork after full days of work or late nights of partying. So be mindful of what is required to get going and stay going. Take this journey seriously.

Do not underestimate the time it takes to fully grasp a new perspective on life.

Your mental, emotional, and physical well-being must be taken seriously to find balance. This balance is what will breed the perception you need to unleash your intuition. Having control over the changeable aspects of your life such as diet, exercise, and financial discipline, should be attended to first. And again, I feel the need to remind you that the results you seek will not be instantaneous. They may take days, weeks, months, or even years to fully develop. Even after three years of constant self-work, sobriety, and discipline, I need to be just as strong today as I was when I started, and that the results I see now are still only the beginning of what my life has to offer. Stay true to fixing your foundations first, and then the things that may be more difficult to manifest like having your dream house or job, retiring early, or finding love will become easier over time. Heroes aren't born holding their phones or scrolling through other people's lives. They are born in the hearts of the tenacious. Be diligent with your daily, weekly, and monthly progress and you will soon make even greater changes than what you ever could have imagined.

I want to understand why I have this deep-rooted sense of guilt.

I always feel like I could be doing more, such as hanging out with friends and family or focusing on my health. I feel like I owe it to myself to get the most out of life and that I owe it to others to spend more time with them because I shunned life to selfishly shovel drugs for years. My guilt is spawned from shame. I am so ashamed of my actions that I feel I need to do what people ask of me, even if it costs me my free time. I feel overwhelmed, which keeps me from relaxing.

But that isn't fair to me. I will run myself into the ground, trying to please everyone. There is a time and place to relax, see loved ones, and vacation. There is also a time to work and grow. Understanding how to balance these things is how to live a happy, fulfilling life. You end up either exhausted, lazy, or regretful when you don't. Planning ahead and knowing that it's okay to say "No" will lighten the load from your weary shoulders and give you the space to heal. Of course, people want to see you and be with you. That's what love is. And don't forget what loving yourself looks and feels like: It looks like you are chasing your dreams and smiling big. Nothing happens overnight. Be persistent. Let your emotions be free when you express yourself, and let your reasoning guide you through your daily duties.

I want to be a positive person but thinking about all the lost souls and how cruel the world can send me into a state of regression – back to the "me" that finds comfort in addiction.

But that's in the past. No longer will I reach for a sense of false hope in something as negative as that. Recognizing our duality and accepting both sides – the positive and the negative – as one and the same is how I find peace. My frantic mind used to be a curse, but with the right training, I am turning it into a blessing.

I used to ask, "Am I the only one who sees the potential of the human race?" Such an open-ended question can have a person chasing their tail for hours only to end in frustration. Now, I no longer need to ask such questions. I no longer need to worry about a life of hypotheticals. I no longer need to hang a cloud of pity over my head. Instead, I will let the rain and sun coat my inner self. I allow the clouds to eclipse all extremes equally. The stars dance even during the day; you just can't see them, so you marvel at night instead. Perspective is everything, and even the darkness of addictions can bring the light of understanding. You can find bliss and anguish in everything, so why fixate on either? Accept and forgive your past, and you will find a willingness to exist to the fullest.

I tell myself I will turn my thoughts and ideas into something and then go on with my life without acting.

I need to take action!

The greatest hell on earth is knowing what you are capable of and then being too weak or lost or afraid to reach for it. If everyone is a slave to *something*, then I am probably a slave to my thoughts and mind. The constant flux of "what-ifs" cripples my impulses. I've let negative, doubtful, pretentious thoughts into my head because I have let other people's biases define me. I have come too far to allow slander and other people's opinions to stop me from being the happiest person I can be. I am blind to the idea that I can willingly let them go, that I am not a slave to my mind. I have to take a stand against the intangible. I have to separate myself from the people in my life who are negative, even if it hurts. You have to keep telling yourself that no matter what, it is for the best. It is difficult to stop the negative thoughts and thinking about memories that hurt, but you can practice letting them pass through you to better enjoy the moment and live authentically.

The world is rotten, or the world can blossom.

I cannot lose faith if I am still a part of it.

If this world wants to crumble beneath me, I will build it anew.

Tragedy finds its way into the hearts of the hopeful to remind them that life is never perfect.

Life is constantly changing along with our perception of it, but as long as we remain hopeful, even when we feel lost, we will find our peace of mind.

Sadness and anger are two sides of the same coin, one that is constantly spinning in the air after time itself has flipped it.

Only when we snatch it to see which side is up, do we express the emotion that the events have called for – and then we give it back to Time to be flipped again. This is not to say we cannot find happiness, for moments of joy are felt only after casting our gaze away from that spinning coin to marvel at the beautiful reality that we craft and perceive.

It's time to put my thoughts at center stage again instead of burying them down where the light cannot shine.

Therefore, I need to shed light on some of the things I ran from, whether my lack of forgiveness, the suppression of my tears and fears, or the shame I haven't dealt with. I'm ashamed that I let the opinions and biases of others poison my mind, heart, and soul to the point where it damaged my sense of self. I'm ashamed I tried to drown my consciousness in a sea of vices. I'm ashamed I closed off my heart from the idea of love to fit the silly narrative of a lonely prisoner. I'm ashamed that I never asked for help. And yet all of these things can be worked on – proof enough that there is something to look forward to. The healing of my shame is something to be proud of.

I have to bounce back.

There is no stopping these events from happening. My life is a constant flux of "get-ups" and "let-downs." Granted, my let-downs now stop at my next wall or barrier regarding creativity and well-being instead of destroying my body and mind with substances like I used to. These stagnant moments allow me to reflect, and I have to learn not just to stop but to slowly move through my trials, learn at a steady pace, reflect, and then act. Once you learn something, your actions with this knowledge make a difference. It then becomes knowledge you have made your own.

As an addict or a substance user, I was always trying to learn the same thing from different angles because I felt like I was missing the one thing causing my failures. I did not have the courage to take action, because deep down, I knew I no longer needed my addictions to experience life, be creative, and think for myself – which meant I would have to get sober and healthy and face my clear mind. Why would I continue to alter my perception of reality to keep learning the same thing differently and not put it into action? This vicious cycle of addiction led to the deterioration of my convictions. And yet the pain was comforting, and it lasted for years. Now the years pass without such thoughts, and I reflect on how the cycle I'm creating now is more well-rounded and straight-forward. When a well is tapped, I shall find a new water vein.

There was a time when I thought I was going to be like you.

Actually, there was a time when I *wanted* to be like you – a you who is more alone than the average person bent on honing their craft, without a love life, and with minimal contact with friends and family. That was the image I believed I needed to chase my dreams. I was toiling away with no distractions. Just me and my thoughts. Just me with my life and my perspective. Oh, how wrong I was! Is that even considered a life? Or a sham cloaked with an undying work ethic and an inability to empathize with anyone but yourself? That is not love, and that will surely not be my life going forward. For if I must trade the basic foundations of healthy relationships with those I love to have a shot at fame, then I would rather be poor, for I know the experiences I share with others are the things that make me, *me*.

Good or bad, what good does it do to toil away in solitude for weeks, months, or years on end while the world and its people pass you by? You cannot write about life if you are too scared to live it. And you cannot preach love and compassion if you are too afraid to face it. I cannot blame this perception of the "committed dreamer" for shunning the world in order to work, but I can blame it for closing my heart. If I were to become the you I had hoped, my art would be stale like the heart that made it. I am the only one to blame for that pretentious attitude, and I will watch that image of "you" wither as I blossom. Your face will fade, while mine stays constant, free, and accepting. Not perfect, but humble enough to know where I fall short. Humble enough to know that I have a heart and that people out there need me.

My parents did a remarkable job instilling selflessness in me.

Sadly, this comes at a cost if not applied correctly. I tended to give everyone the benefit of the doubt, even if it came at the expense of them taking advantage of me. Why? Because I wanted to give them a chance to be real, better, and become loving people. Because making people smile is the best feeling in the world. Because laughter, a helping hand, or being there for someone is the greatest of human achievements. But I was naïve, and my earnestness was ultimately self-destructive. The belief I had that shallow, selfish people have good hearts deep down destroyed me. My endless compassion to help them got the better of me more times than not. I became people's punching bag because I knew I could take it. I knew I was tough. I thought I could handle it. I was wrong.

I buried my pain and became hateful and malicious to defend myself from a world I let walk all over me. Instead of forgiving myself, I sought to punish myself for ever thinking I could help someone in that way. And I was right to realize this, but I failed to understand that I had to forgive myself for keeping moving forward. We hold these failures deep in our hearts because we feel like we could have done things differently for the people we care about. We sometimes forget that the best support is the support we give ourselves. Only now have I realized that I must become the version of myself that loves instead of hates. I cannot give up on helping people; I just need to figure out a healthy way to do it.

We compare ourselves to others and how they spend their time instead of just using our time in our way to the fullest.

I am no expert, for I always learn the hard way that I let people affect me too much. Not only what they say about me but what they say about others and how they react to the world and its biases. I have been too easily molded by the people of this planet instead of following my heart. It is not that spending time with others is holding me back; instead, I need to learn not to take things personally when people comment about situations they don't understand. Only then will I find peace because the institutions of modern man have been altered to separate us and fill us with insecurity when they should be creating a culture of learning and understanding. We focus too much on what makes us different and then envy and/or judge other people's accomplishments and shortcomings. Technology has given us the ability to see the richest and the poorest humans without providing context on how they got to the position they are in. We are fearful of the worst, and we idolize the grand. There is no common work ethic or authenticity to push us forward – only biases of inequality and paranoia divide us further. Come back to your instincts, your roots. Remember how we should treat each other while caring for your well-being and moral compass.

There was a time when I thought my loneliness was a curse – the universe's way of punishing me for not loving myself.

Why should I enjoy the company of others if I am unable to enjoy my own? I also thought that this was where I had to do all my work – in solitude, where my thoughts are free and unhinged, free from the dogma that has distorted this beautiful world. But over time, I became stale, and my perception became so fragile that I did not know how to exist in reality. I was falling apart, and all I could do to cope was turn on every screen while filling my cup with addictions. "Leave me alone," I used to think. Let me rot, for I do not deserve love or a future. Then I finally realized the limits of my perception, which is no less true while I've been sober. The loneliness I felt while hiding from the triggers that accompanied my friends and family masked my need to learn to love myself. It is not a punishment to be alone; it is a punishment to be alone and not love yourself. It is a blessing to be alone and understand what self-love is.

Earth to Jon: If there were something you loved doing, you would stop at nothing to do it, no matter how busy you are.

Your passions should not take a back seat to your obligations; they should ride beside them. How long will depression and suicide be an excuse for why you do not chase your dreams? How long will you continue to make excuses for your lack of progress and vigor while simultaneously choosing to be a slave to negative habits and perspectives? Deep down, you are afraid of failing. But this is baseless and irrational. You didn't fear failing when you were at the height of your substance abuse. Granted, there wasn't much to fail at. Your only measure of success was acquiring enough substances. You had no respect for your own life and the outcome of your choices. You had no respect for how the world works and then played victim to issues you already had the answers for.

If you want to continue going against the grain and hating the process, you will drift into comfort and mediocrity. Instead, embrace what makes you both unique and uncomfortable if you really want to relate with those who are broken – like you. This is not to say that depression and suicide aren't valid excuses for not wanting to chase your dreams, but if that is what you genuinely want to do, spend the time and money to find professional help. Not every family or friend will understand the complexities of a mind that's been chasing its tail. It may feel humbling, but seeking help and focusing on your health before chasing your dreams is okay.

If you want something to change, don't rely on someone else to change it for you.

There is no guarantee it will be the change you want.

There are two things I know: We will not find the answers through our phones or television screens, and we must craft solutions within our perspectives and put them to work through our day-to-day actions. If we, as a species, are truly supposed to come together, now is the time. There is no other reason to be in this position than to face the fact that we must learn to respect each other. We can all point fingers and place blame, but the truth is that we did this to ourselves. No one is innocent. People struggle, and people make mistakes. But the worst thing we can do is cut ourselves off from the world to punish ourselves. We forget that there are lots of people like us out there. We need to remind each other that we are all in this together. Don't hole up in your "sanctuary." Find the time to be productive and healthy, and then share that enthusiasm with those around you. Initiative spreads like wildfire, and the people of this world are waiting to make this planet a better place.

The day you stop fantasizing and start planning is the day your dreams begin to become reality.

It is easy to visualize but more difficult to choose and initiate actions. Even if our plan is incomplete, start somewhere with a couple of steps and figure out the rest as you go forward. There is no procedure for how each unique individual will attain their sought-after lifestyle. No book will do the work for you. It's your plan and your moves. Even if your plan misses a few steps, don't get discouraged. Do not get anxious. The universe will give us enough time to complete what we are here to do as long as we make an effort and give it our best shot. I have never heard a story of someone living their dream and regretting it in the end because they failed too many times on the way there. Become the resilient hero you visualize in your dreams. It's time to quit fantasizing and start taking action.

In this day and age, we rarely meet obstacles that prohibit us from moving forward.

Death itself may be the only thing standing in the way of cultivating our potential and accomplishments. Failing a class, getting fired, being rejected by a crush, or losing a loved one may feel like definitive failures that can't possibly be reconciled, but life is too short to cry about the little things and too long to cry about the big things. This leads me to believe that there is a misconception about forgiveness.

Forgiveness is applied at three different levels: Forgiving yourself, forgiving others, and forgiving the world. You may need to forgive yourself for how you have treated yourself and others or how you've reacted to certain situations in life. You may need to forgive others for the way they have treated you. Lastly, we may feel as though we need to forgive the world because we think the world has wronged us. This third situation, however, overlaps with the first reason because our perception has created an illusion that has us playing victim to the whims of the world. Still, it is easier just to forgive the world because the universe happens at its own pace, without regard for anyone. Simply make your peace and be on your way.

Forgiveness doesn't mean things go back to the way they were. What's done is done. Forgiveness means accepting the sincerity of an apology or the situation's outcome and accepting that no one is perfect. Mistakes happen, and people deserve second chances – or at least your empathy and guidance. None of this warrants forgetfulness, though; if you think you can let things go back to how they were, you will only get hurt again. Learn from your mistakes, forgive them, and learn from others' mistakes.

There is no guarantee that everything will work out how you want it to.

There isn't even a guarantee that if you put all of your effort into something, it will work out in the end. I can tell you, though, that putting 5% into visualization, another 5% into actual work, and the remaining 90% into "I will get to it later" *definitely* won't work. This goes for everything in life: relationships, hobbies, dreams, and goals. Nothing is guaranteed, so you might as well give it 100% no matter what. That way, if it worked out, you knew you had it in you. And if you fail, you know you did your best and can proudly get up and try again. You'll only know it won't work when you are six feet under. As long as you draw breath, there is still time. The purpose of life is to make the best of what you have. I am no longer a victim of my addictions. They are now a strength, not a weakness.

Honesty is the most potent medicine for the soul.

It is amazing to realize that a simple conversation with oneself or a loved one can completely change the rhythm of the mind. Yet out in the world, we get cold feet because we are living through our screens. Looking someone in the eye – or even at their face – often makes people uncomfortable, as if strangers to our emotions. Coming to terms with our health choices, career paths, or relationships is something we'll put on the back burner until it's too late. We know deep down that we lose ourselves each day and that we don't stay true to our most authentic wishes. But no one said this was going to be easy. All we can do is trust in our judgements and lean on our loved ones who have supported us through it all. Be honest with yourself and have that conversation. Facing our insecurities and doubts with words of reassurance and affirmation will lighten the weight we place on our hearts.

I am not perfect.

I only strive to be a version of myself that is capable of inspiring other people. To aid in their healing may involve talking about the reasons I'm not perfect, which involve substance abuse, depression, anxiety, shame, failure, and ungratefulness, and reasons I tried to run from. But I ended up running in a circle back to the beginning and the pain that started it all. Remind me yet again why I lost the ability to forgive myself. Remind me yet again how I hurt those around me. This is the conversation I need to have with myself that will help me heal first, so I'll be able to help others.

I am not an evil person, though the jaded opinions of others about me did take root in my mind, and I let these thoughts punish me. Oh, how I loved to beat myself up for it, wishing I could atone for my mistakes. Instead of forgiving myself, I drove my soul deeper and deeper into the ground, hoping something positive will sprout later, that for now, this dirt suits me because that's what I am: Nothing but dirt. And the more I told myself this, the more I believed it. The more I believed it, the longer it took me to forgive myself for it. "I am not dirt, or worthless, or evil," I told myself on the first day I got sober. "I am not perfect. But I am beautiful, I am love, and I can dream of a better life." Now it's time for the actual work, and thankfully that seed was planted a long time ago – a belief that took form and grew thanks to my efforts to heal through sobriety. Now I see. Now I see what I truly need to be. The journey has only just begun.

I am scared, even if I act like I'm not.

This is my last obstacle – the last checkpoint before I re-enter the world, ready, willing, and healed. There is no turning back once I face this. It's the last prerequisite before starting my master plan of finally attaining a sturdy foundation of mental and physical well-being. But why am I dragging my feet? Because this final lock will ask a lot from me.

To be scared of the future – the unknown and the loss of a past self – is genuinely terrifying. As humans, we are frightened at the idea of losing what makes us comfortable. Our past and the habits and coping mechanisms that accompany it are all we know. By healing ourselves and moving on, we will shed that skin while heading into a future of uncertainty. But our pasts will never truly leave us. We cannot outrun these thoughts; all we can do is let them pass through. People think that not having regrets means never thinking about the thoughts that haunt you, but they couldn't be further from the truth. Those thoughts will always be there, ready to remind you of your failures and the miseries of life. There is no such thing as a future without a past, and there is no present without accepting the possibilities of the future and the consequences of the past. Every thought in existence, whether malicious, shameful, enlightening, or full of love, still exists in the minds of every human, whether they want to believe it or not.

The human condition is endless. And instead of holding back for fear of being ostracized, it's time to express our authentic truth – in words and actions entirely. Those who face the grand landscape known as eternal nothingness will have to tread lightly, for even the most headstrong will drop at the sheer weight of their circumstances. Do not tremble, falter, or avert your eyes. Cast them towards the prism known as consciousness and be born anew.

Part Two

Hope

The visualization has been given life, the discomfort has been shed, and the light of perspective has grown brighter.

With the groundwork for a better tomorrow having been laid out, we can now take action. We can finally become the person we've been dreaming to be.

There is now *Hope*.

As the journey becomes open to all the possibilities we are ready to take, our mindsets and lives become magnets for vigor, gratitude, and opportunity. We must stay vigilant in pursuing a positive mindset as the consequences of our previous actions and life's misfortunes can still weaken even the strongest people. We must keep reminding ourselves of why we set out on this path in the first place.

This is the culmination of all our hard work and struggles – it is now who we are. It's easy to *speak* of our dreams and our plans, but now we must face the hardest part of our journey: living them fully. We have trained our perspectives and souls to be resilient against our doubts and the world's temptations. Our loved ones and peers have been witnesses to our spurts of greatness, with cheers of reassurance to keep us strong and on the path, we have chosen.

The following parables and essays are a bit more abstract,

representing the subjective inspiration we need to continue our progress and persist on our journey. In finishing this gift to you, I have revitalized myself to keep my head up through the coming days. The world is scary for some of us, but that doesn't mean it needs to stay that way.

Let us take action together and transmute our feelings of uncertainty into the unwavering courage we know we deserve.

Hope is something that lives in sync with the seasons.

The growth, decay, and re-rooting of dreams become part of our transformation when we let ourselves become one with nature and its cycles. We can either watch those cycles unfold or unfold with them and experience every aspect. The leaves and flowers that spring forth give us hope as we trust our instincts. The bright sun glistens with beauty as our souls radiate energy. The changing colors of the seasons remind us of the need to change our perspective when others have run their course. The silent fall of the sky's flurries gives us rest as we attempt a metamorphosis yet again. Breathing with this world, we again become one with our destiny.

What, then, should we do with the synchronicities we experience or the assimilation of new knowledge? Why we can finally live to the fullest! Cast aside the shackles of modernity and return to where you belong: Imagination, freedom, and authenticity. Be grateful for the reminders the universe gives us in our darkest days, lighting the way back to our innate wisdom. "Destiny" may be an I, but the future starts as a blank slate. Day by day, our soul slowly chisels away our conditioning to reveal our truest intentions, our deepest desires, and our most decisive choices. Let us enjoy every step. Let us become what we are destined to be.

I wake up with the intention of bettering myself, whole-heartedly believing that I can make a difference in my life. To that end, I must embrace my tenacity and my passion. It is time for the wildfire in me that was responsible for my past destruction to now bring light and warmth to those around me. There is a brighter tomorrow as long as I can share smiles and laughs with my fellow travelers. For, at last, I have realized that my hard work is paying off. Finally, the fruits of my tireless labor are ripening with results and positivity. I hope that by sharing this harvest, I can sway more people into cultivating their own garden of self-love, health, development, and gratitude. Maybe it's not too late to save this planet and all its creatures, to worry about more than our phones, shows, jobs, and homes. We just have to wake up and better ourselves, to Learn, Create, Provide, and Enlighten. Anything other than the same mindset that has led us into the rut we are in. Drop the propaganda and separatism. Malicious intent must rot where it belongs – in the past with the leaders of old. We have everything we need in order to create a better future; all we must do is take action. Remember where you started, what you worked through, who you are, and who you want to become. Now go.

Don't forget to tell yourself, "Good job."

It is easy to be hard on ourselves with so many expectations in this world from our families, peers, jobs, and government – much of it with no regard for who we want to be. Just keep answering with the same generic response and orthodoxically acceptable career path and lifestyle. But know that this makes it even harder to praise our efforts when we do things solely for ourselves. Our health, our hobbies, and especially our well-being will take a back seat to the conditions laid out by the media and technology – which only creates a vicious cycle of overwork and doubt, making it easy to be hard on myself and difficult to praise my efforts when I do well.

However, I cannot accomplish greatness in a day, which is humbling. I know that sounds ridiculous, but in all honesty, I rarely feel that I have done enough. I hold myself to too high a standard because I feel I need to make up for "lost time" – time I "wasted" being addicted to drugs, alcohol, and technology. But time is only wasted if you believe it is, and now I know that I went through all the hard times for a reason: to learn and document my experience. And that was hard work. I've worked hard to earn these years of sobriety. I've worked hard for my degree. I've worked hard to be able to write.

Everyone has accomplishments they are proud of, no matter how grand or small they may be. We must remind ourselves of these successes, for by forgetting them, we open the door to be even harder on our progress and potentially slip back into madness. It is even more important to be grateful for our relationships and our health. Learn to praise your own efforts instead of looking outside for validation. There is no need to brag or gloat; simply own your achievements and share them as you are moved to with the rest of the world. You are enough; you've done a good job so far. Clarity, happiness, health, and financial stability are waiting for you.

People give me hope. Love gives me hope.

Being around people or consoling them motivates me to be a better person. Because when I hear myself talking about the habits and perspectives, I think other people should have to improve their lives, it gives me even more incentive to do those same things. I know I can be a better person and conquer my fears; I just have to talk to myself the way I speak to others who need me. It's always difficult to practice what we preach because we often mistake our counsel to others for better behavior, thinking we have already accomplished the feat ourselves! Then a false pride rears its ugly head. The solution is to take action, for only when we achieve our own results can we legitimately guide others. And in sharing those accomplishments, we spur others to seek their own. But be careful in how you share. Avoid political, moral, or religious views and focus on the importance of self-worth and self-love.

Keep telling yourself you can do it.

No matter what your goal or how impossible it may seem, never lose hope. For if we let our doubts overtake us, we will surely slip into complacency. It may *seem* impossible to be addicted to a plethora of deadly substances and habits and then become – and stay – sober, but I am proof positive that it's not! Some may think it's impossible to become a successful musician, singer, or artist. Others think it's impossible to lose the weight they've put on for decades or quit a years-long smoking habit. I can tell you that nothing is impossible that has already been done by others. Of course, we can't fly or live forever – gravity and mortality must be reckoned with. But by facing the goals that *are* possible, we internalize the possibility: the possibility to become healthier, to acquire a better job or financial situation, to build up your relationships and friendships, even to love yourself. Identify your "possibles" and tell yourself each day that you can achieve them until by sheer determination they happen!

I was tired of crying about things I knew I could change.

Why come home and make the same choices over and

over if I know I'll regret them later and end up hating myself? I knew I could get sober; I just didn't know whether it needed to be permanent (it did!). I knew I could graduate college; I just needed a clear mind to do so. I knew I could finally trust my writing again – once I learned to love and forgive myself. I knew I was capable of eating healthy foods and exercising regularly; I just needed to accept that it was going to be harder than I anticipated. I was tired of having the answers and not knowing what to do with them. Where to start? When to start? Right now would be perfect!

I believe the word "perfect" – which to me means "complete and unassailable" – is only appropriate when used for the exact instance you decide to start living your life authentically and to the fullest with the purest intentions. What can perfection really describe other than the transcendence of the human spirit? Even though my methods aren't perfect and my processes are rough around the edges, the only thing I ask to be perfect is my unshakeable tenacity in the present moment. Even if those moments of perfect tenacity come and go, I hope I can fully experience their beauty. I cannot change the setbacks of my past, but I know I can change the things that destroy me. I can change how I anticipate future consequences. How? By taking the right action in each moment. Understand what you can and cannot do and build a sturdy foundation. Then you can stop crying and truly start living.

For the first time in my life, I can honestly say that I am looking forward to a hopeful future.

I am excited and even ecstatic. I am grateful for the present moment. For the hard work, I've put in. For the beautiful people and opportunities, I've been blessed with. I now realize that the universe was never against me; it was always me against myself. In fact, the universe lives within me, so I was fighting myself and the universe simultaneously! My disappointments and dissatisfactions were rooted in my inability to be grateful for being alive. Finally, after toiling to remove my vices and weaknesses, I can see a brighter future. My ideas are flowing again. My health has improved. I am financially stable. Life is good! I hope this feeling lasts forever, and I will do anything to protect it. I will do everything I can to share it. I want it to reach the hearts of those who need a reminder that there are still good people in this world. We may seem lost at times, but we have the ability to change and conquer – anything!

Life begins to unthaw while the sounds of spring rise over the roar of city streets.

The winter months took a significant toll on many as we waited patiently for a new day to give us hope. Even with the world in disarray, we try our best to wake up and smile. Be strong for the little ones who don't understand yet. Let them have the same carefree imagination we did before technology took hold of our innocence. Oh spring, please bring a truly new beginning this year. The last two years have been hard at best. I will do my part. I will burst forth this spring. I will be the sprout that waited under the snow for the birds to chirp. I will bring dreams of being the biggest tree around, big enough to shade the world when the sun gets too hot, when the air is too heavy with pollution, offering refuge for my brothers and sisters from a planet in peril. I will be there to help revitalize them with the energy of a new season. Nature doesn't need to "come together," for it is already in unity. If we are to learn anything from where we came from, it must be our affinity for togetherness. Like roots, we are connected as one nervous system for one cause. Let us remember our purpose and enjoy spring in the spirit it intends for us – renewal!

Positivity and hope are best experienced with persistence.

One must learn to harness it, to find a way each day to remind yourself of the option – the need – to be positive. We get lost in our miseries, then end the day with the same vague intention to start the next anew. We are worth more than this. We deserve better, and so does this planet. We deserve a better perspective! We deserve to breathe freely! We deserve to have a calm mind! We deserve to love our lives! Do not forget that you deserve to be loud about it as well!

There's a difference between the time you put into your creative energy and the activities you want to make routine because they are healthy habits.

We all have activities or hobbies, which comes with the ever-expansive world of the 21st century. Unfortunately, as we grow older, we get better at coming up with reasons to stop doing our favorite hobbies. I believe the biggest reason has to do with not having enough time or not managing the time we have. After working our mundane jobs to pay the bills and survive, it's hard to muster up the energy necessary to do the things we love. So instead, we find some type of screen or substance to entertain us. I believe the second reason is that we become too self-conscious of what others will think if we continue such "silly" hobbies as art, music, dancing, theater – anything "out of the box" or untraditional.

As children, we did whatever we wanted because it was fun, different, and exciting, driven by our imagination and energy for new experiences. Over time, however, life trained us to become so focused on building a stable foundation that we chiseled away the abstract, the free, and the innocence. The third reason for not doing the things we love is, for me, the worst: because they don't make us money. We've been conditioned to need/love money to maintain our social status and accumulate new things, and it has infected us mentally and emotionally.

These three reasons also interfere with our need to exercise and eat correctly. We forget that the territory of personal progress includes living a better and more fulfilled life which requires continued effort – effort piled on top of our already demanding careers and lives. I can promise you, though, it's all still possible. You just need to start limiting the activities that make you lazy and steadily introduce dieting, exercise, and other positive hobbies into your life. It won't happen overnight, even though technology has given us the impression that we can attain anything we want with the push of a button. These accomplishments will require more than just the swipe/tap of a thumb or the click of a mouse. Take a step back and remember what it feels like to be yourself without the screens, biases, or usual activities. Try living a "new life."

Do things to increase the quality of your *perception* of life.

Notice that I didn't say, "quality of life," because that may be confused with acquiring material objects, which may feel nice at first but will fade over time, leaving you wanting more. You will chase that gratification, and it will distract you from life's true beauty. Go for a walk, grab a coffee with a friend, listen to music, dance, read a book, or pick up an old hobby. Such things will always be more fulfilling than material accumulation because you are directly appreciating your ability to enjoy life instead of seeking to enjoy life by acquiring a nice object.

This is not to say that buying nice, new things as a reward for hard work is bad, for that would make me a hypocrite! But my life doesn't revolve around it. Some of those things will inevitably lose their appeal, and you will likely attempt to fill that void with still more objects, creating a savage cycle of discontent and greed. Find authentic, genuine value in activities and people, and your perception of life will expand. You'll be surprised at how good it feels to smile when you don't even realize you're happy. Maybe that's what they call heaven.

Everyone gets to their own heaven their own way.

There is no perfect path to the pearly gates. All you can do is get there the best you can. You can't change other people's minds on how to get there or what their heaven will actually look like. It is too subjective to even debate. Regardless of what "proof" the world wants to lay on you, just stay centered and positive. Head towards wherever it is that you are going with a smile, and you might be inclined to believe that you were in heaven all along!

I've been uncertain about my feelings toward "love" for much of my adult life, though I certainly preach it to others. This is mostly because I began hating myself because of my addictions and past failures. Most people think of love as romantic love or familial love, but for the sake of exploration, let's consider love as an affection towards something or someone. This can mean the love for yourself, your family, your spouse, your hobbies, your friends, or our planet. I had become uncertain about love because I had lost my love for them all. I believed I deserved no forgiveness, and as punishment would be cursed to walk this earth in search of a feeling that doesn't exist to fill that void.

These last couple of months have taught me that this perception of my need to be punished is – how shocking – wrong! Strangely enough, I am no longer surprised by such revelations, though I am humbled yet again. Slowly but surely, this old heart of mine returns to the sleeve that once clothed an absence of joy. I realize that compassion has boundaries, and this time I will stay strong in my conviction to aid others. I will not let this world, or its villains, bring me down again. If I'm to be here, then I must become love. I must become strong enough to learn to love myself and all of my imperfections. There is no reason to let my hate for the ugliness in this world ruin my daily life. I must forgive myself, and I must move forward."

Love is a strange thing.

Of all the things we experience in life, I don't feel as though I'm addicted to it like I was for other substances

– even now when I have it. You can become addicted to anything; don't be fooled by what others tell you. But something about love is different. I respect its distance and am grateful for its presence. It's a reassuring comfort and something I want to share. It should not be taken for granted, for when you do, you will quickly learn your mistake! So treasure it instead, but don't feel hopeless without it. You are still capable of living a fulfilling life on your own while embodying the essence of love.

Time allows love to slow down or speed up our perception of reality. Learning how to harness that throttle is how to live in the moment. When you think about it, love is the most versatile and resilient element in existence! It can be applied to any situation with the intention of bettering it. Of course, love isn't perfect either, as it can infect us with obsessive behaviors. Too much of anything even love! can be "a bad thing." The challenge is how to react to balance our relationship with love: easing up on the throttle if we become too obsessive or putting our foot on the gas when we start becoming apathetic. Once you do, your life will blossom. Maintain a stable composure and a welcoming mind, and you will soon be living your best life.

Love and hope come in many different forms.

Whether it's a new connection with someone or an experience outside of the usual, the universe sends different types of love through many different people and activities to remind us why we should be loving ourselves and our time more. So always be open to letting potential new loves in.

Your heart gives you life. Your brain gives meaning to that life.

Do not underestimate the power of a healthy mind and body. A clear and well-managed mind, coupled with a healthy diet for your heart and body, will do wonders for any internal turmoil that arises from misunderstanding how to react to the world around you.

Life is simpler than we make it out to be.

The courage to hope lies within yourself.

Stop looking to other sources to bring you peace. The media, the news, platforms for social life, and even the world of entertainment won't get you peace or take you any closer to figuring yourself out or finding the tranquility to face your desperation. No amount of food, drugs, or stimuli will calm your soul. Everything that exists outside of you has nothing to do with how you ultimately react internally. Only by courageously confronting your doubts and insecurities will you find the perspective to tackle the vices that are keeping you from blossoming. Stand firm and become your salvation.

You are capable of anything.

To find something worth crying for that is also worth dying for may be the most fulfilling experience you have.

Embrace those moments and those experiences, whatever they may be; they are priceless despite the losses, which can be the toughest and most emptying feeling of all. There is no guarantee we will get over such loss; we may also never be blessed with what we truly desire. But that is the calling card of life, yes? That uncertainty pushes us to strive, to reach, to hope, and in those moments of struggle, we truly feel alive. For if we always received everything we desired, would we not grow bored with our journey? Would we wake up with vigor and ambition or loaf around knowing there is nothing left to do?

I tell you this: Nothing is guaranteed.

Your happiness, your health, your dreams, your salvation, and your heaven are all in the hands of the unspoken unknown. All the signs in existence still couldn't paint a picture of certainty for your future. All we can do is give life everything we have: all of our effort, our love, our thoughts, our feelings, and our work. Everything we are in any given moment must be fully expressed to *possibly* achieve our dreams. Possibly? Am I telling you that things still might not work out? Yep! So give it 110% anyway! At least you can cry along the way and tell yourself it was good to be alive regardless of the ending. Wake up and be relentless. Strive, cry, die, sleep, laugh, love, and fly to the greatest heights and live there with your dreams. Find something to cry for. Find something to die for. Find something to fly for.

Use experience to block out hesitation.

Continue to do whatever it is that moves you closer to enjoying your life. The more often you fail, the easier it gets later to overcome any obstacle. The "loading bar" – the accumulation of time and effort that you put into achieving a goal – will slowly but surely move you closer to achievement. Progress may creep slowly or look like it's not even moving, but rest assured, you are on the way. Hard work isn't rewarded with dial-up connectivity; it's rewarded with fiber optics!

The speed at which you complete your trials today are exponentially greater than the speed it took previously. You may hesitate at times, and that's okay. It took me nearly eight years of failing miserably to finally take sobriety seriously. It took me ten years to graduate from college, and twelve years to publish my first song and my first book. Whatever accomplishment is most important to you, I promise that you can achieve it. No matter how many days, months, or years it takes, the experience and effort you put in today will blossom into something beautiful. I am living proof of that, and I hope you can become living proof to yourself as well.

The world you create for yourself is only doomed if you allow it to be.

Look inwards for the hope that you have the ability to create and protect your own kingdom. There are so many competing sources of information and opinions that it's hard to stay true to ourselves. It's easy to look outward for signs that we are on the right path, and sometimes we see them, but sometimes they disappear or mislead us. So don't look to your screens for answers; you will only become a slave to their glow. Remember that compassion and love will make any situation more easily understood and traversed. Look inward to find out what you should be doing to live a better life.

It's how we get up after being knocked down that defines who we are.

Whether it was a self-inflicting stream of bad decisions that set us back or unfortunate events we weren't prepared to deal with, how we respond and react to these situations will determine whether or not we become stronger. I believe that the only thing that makes a genius is that they never give up. Never giving up is the most indispensable tool to take on a mission.

I promise to no longer be ashamed of myself.

I have put in the work to back this up, and I believe this is a promise I can now faithfully keep. No longer will I be ashamed of who I am, the thoughts I've had, or the things I've done. I will be proud of myself, not from pride itself but because I realize I'm just as flawed as anyone and yet continue to work through my shortcomings. In this humility, I find the right to be alive. For once in my life, I will give myself credit for my hard work instead of criticizing how it should have been done sooner or worrying about what needs to be done next. For today marks the birth of a new me – the me who has finally conquered my many deadly habits with enough intensity and energy left to tell the world it is possible. Whatever you are dreaming or thinking, good intentions, forgiveness, mental and physical well-being, and compassion are some of the simple yet forgotten themes you'll need to reach your goals and fully understand your place in the universe.

For far too long, I let society's expectations bury me alive beneath numbing coping mechanisms. I became ashamed that I even allowed such a thing to happen, and then I became ashamed that I was too lazy and weak to change anything. No longer. This time, this day, and this moment will become mine entirely. No government, religion, cell phone, teacher, friend, boss, parent, individual, or institution will be able to take this moment, and this feeling, away from me. My decisions and accomplishments are now mine to hold. My efforts, insights, and self-work will pave the way to a better tomorrow.

There is no *Eureka* moment that shifts the blueprint of our mind and soul into perfect alignment that makes the changes to fix our lives.

There is no magical force in the universe that will stand you up to do whatever it takes to make you a better person. Such work is reserved for the relentless and the authentic. Such work can be exhausting, but the results lead to the greatest feeling of all. My sobriety has created a version of myself that is barely comparable to the man I once was, although that broken version of myself always visualized the man I am today. You have to start somewhere, so find whatever it is you are looking for in this book or, more importantly, within yourself and get to work!

My three main reasons for wanting sobriety:
1. I was tired of not living my life to the fullest.
2. My health was in decline.
3. I knew that an unfiltered perspective would clear a path to greatness.

The demons that used to control me are now part of my army. For those of you fighting similar or other demons, you may be saying, "Well, I don't need to be completely [sober]; I just need to get a couple of bad habits under control." And that is perfectly fine. My purpose in stating my reasons for doing what I did is to emphasize how the effort has blessed me with an entirely new perspective and energy for life. Those who hope to live their dreams don't need to go to the extremes I did. I only share my story in hopes of helping others find their motivation and courage. Everyone has inner demons or thought cycles that cause pain, suffering, and addiction. You can continue to deny the existence of your power to overcome them or use that power to create a new perspective and channel that energy into living a better life.

The future is an illusion.

The past is a crumbling statue.

The present is a blossoming flower of choices.

Let this current moment burst forth with possibility. Let whatever it is that drives you to improve to take control. Become whatever you envision yourself to be. Find a rhythm or an image of yourself doing what you love. Now make it a reality, make it happen in the realm you breathe, not solely the one where you sleep. Make plans, cut ties, take action. We overcomplicate things because the human mind wanders into endless possibilities. It doesn't help that media overload has bombarded us with an excess of "what-if" scenarios that cloud our every decision. Take a break from the digital world and find solace in the reality where your physical self exists. This is where all the magic happens.

Do not lose hope, young warriors.

The consciousness we have all been blessed with is something spectacular. I know it is easier to hide in your shell than to face this world, but we have to remember how capable we truly are. We were given no tools to cope with this ever-changing reality. They did not teach us balance in school. Society tells you to drink or party on the weekend to ease the pain from the work week. But how well does that really work? Is that really life? You are different than that, are you not?

We are different than that! We don't need to numb our passions just to get through the week. We can find a balance of pleasure and health; we just need to try. Only by learning how to balance your emotions and thoughts will you be rewarded with something priceless – clarity. Realign the stars in your eyes into a vivid picture of magnificence. Maybe now you won't tuck your tail when you see an opportunity. Perhaps you will start to remember why you came here in the first place. This is a rite of passage into the vastness of existence. Your existence. Something even you can be proud of.

My hands are ripping through the fabric of my cocoon.

I can finally see the light of day, and it warms my face beyond measure. I am so close to this new life that I can taste the air of a new land. A new time. One not restricted by the responsibilities of the modern human. A mind that is no longer plagued like the modern human. I have been waiting for this new land and new time since the moment I tore down the curtains made of lies. No longer shall I use my behaviors or circumstances as an excuse for why I was blind. I leap so gallantly I might as well be a gazelle, running the savannah as the sun sets, surrounded by the calming beauty of nature. This is where I need to be: away from this concrete jungle. This is why I receded to my cocoon – to wait, patiently, for the moment of my rebirth. It is close, and my entire being awaits the maelstrom of experience waiting on the other side. I cry, but these are tears of joy, not fear, for I've finally redeemed myself. I smile. So close. I can have it. This infinity. This life. This story. This love.

Mother Nature peels away my tainted flesh as I walk through this forest on a winding path.

I stop to feel and see the sun shimmer on the river. My loneliness used to make me regretful and full of shame, but this time it's different. Transcending the monotony of society through sobriety will bring a blinding light to my purpose, binding me to a fate filled with philosophy, forgiveness, and smiling and becoming the thing that most are too scared to be—sacrificing the comfort zones that hold unlocked potential. Never waver, never falter. Universal love needs no alter – only a heart to set everything ablaze. From your guilt-ridden past to the tears you hide, let it all go. Don't be afraid to be alone.

Readers, this cocoon you sit in is preparing you for wings to spread the truth. Never doubt yourself because of the things people have said to you. Do not hate or hold a grudge against them either. Do not seek vengeance on a world that is already dying because you blame the government for the reason we are crying. If you truly intend to be wise, to bear the burden of hope that most cannot fathom, you may have to be alone. You may have to be sober. You may have to wear your mangled heart on your sleeve even when you are terrified of getting hurt. You may have to do all these things until the day you die. Is that not what you signed up for, though, all those years ago? Or will you back down and wallow in mediocrity? Wallow in the drugs as you watch the trees and animals burn?

I think not! You may be broken, but if there is one thing you are not, it's defeated. You've already gone past the point of no return. I have seen you acknowledge that – and then smile. If you want to help those who have felt like you, you will have to change your attitude. Gratitude, like sadness, goes a long way. Just make sure you find some balance this time.

It is time to strum a new tune – an entirely new sound that I can jam to.

Me, a broken man, who used to preach about the importance of love and yet hated the world. The victim. The one who is always right while hating everything about himself.

All for pride, so he can keep saying he was done wrong by this world. That way, he will always have an excuse for not fixing himself. Waiting until the tune he's been playing goes stale, when no one, not even him, is dancing any longer. But what to do now? The silence is deafening, though my thoughts are louder than ever. I must remember – no, *we* must remember – who we are. We have forgotten our true nature, the one the earth, stars, and universe gave to us: We are Love. We are not perfect. We are together.

This world and its institutions have divided us against each other and against ourselves. We are numb, overstimulated, and stagnant to the flow of the universe. The institutions of the future may already be here, but that doesn't mean we should allow them to control us. We must learn from our mistakes and create a better future for the ones to come. This new tune will be heard across time, but how do we write it? How do we create a better future? How do we reconnect with ourselves, our brethren, and our planet? We must keep reminding ourselves about the importance of love, under-standing, communication, and sovereignty. We can think for ourselves and calmly converse about life as it is. Caring about our physical, emotional, mental, and communal well-being is infectious and a necessary step to taking back our species and our planet.

Let us find love, together.

Epilogue

I promise you that the doubts we have in respect to our dreams are meaningless.

The world may tell you that having doubts is realistic because it keeps us from taking risks or making dangerous decisions that might hurt others or ourselves. I am here to tell you that the risks you take, and the failures of your choices, are what drive you to succeed! Don't give up on your dreams because you're afraid of the risks. Assuming the worst, without also hoping for the best, will only end in stagnancy and complacency. No one ever said that this journey would be easy, and if we are to suffer, then I hope we suffer while intending to reach a happier place.

We started our perilous journey into infinity with the goal to better ourselves and use our imaginations to visualize what it would be like to be the dream versions of ourselves. Ready and willing to change, we took our first step towards healing and recovery, only to realize that the burden of doing so left us lonely, afraid, and exhausted. With nowhere else to turn, we turned to ourselves in hopes that our own minds would be our saving grace during these times of turmoil. With our backs against the wall, we changed our perspectives to better suit our adaptable human nature and the ever-changing landscape of reality. Reinvigorated and awakened, we walked headstrong into the future in a spirit of love, trust, forgiveness, and hope. This world was never against us; it was always us against ourselves.

So, don't be discouraged when your results are few as you start on the path. The road to health and well-being will not dazzle you with epic achievements and flashy experiences. It is quietly accompanied by tranquility, smiles, and gratefulness for the lives we've been given.

Even years into my sobriety and recovery, I find myself learning new ways to be more present in my quest to forgive myself and grateful for the opportunities to grow.

Be diligent with your goals and compassionate towards your progress, and I promise that good things will come to you. There is no timetable for success, happiness, or health.

Remember: It's a daily battle, and those who are victorious sleep soundly at night knowing they will tackle the next day with the same hope they had the previous day.

Lost

I saw a demon, hunched over on the side of the road.

Who knew that hell had homeless?

But then again,

Hell is hopeless.

"Spare some change," he asked.

"Anything helps."

I stopped and looked,

The place where his heart should be,

An empty crater.

Eyes wishing for a savior.

"I have nothing to give," I replied.

"Only sin remains of me."

He laughed, then pointed to the heart-shaped light,

Dangling from my neck.

"That thing is barely lit," he chuckled.

"I traded mine for this hole.

I no longer feel sorrow or woe,

I simply cling to what I used to know."

"To each his own," I replied.

"I cannot give up hope."

The demon smiled and turned,

Curled into a ball,

As "good luck" carried on a whisper.

I tread on.

Wishing for a breather,

But the only breath I take dries my throat.

A barren wasteland creature.

"Good sir, if I may have a moment of your time?"

I look up to see a demon,

Horns through a shabby cap.

A conman, an empty dreamer.

"What say we make a trade?

Hearts like that are rare you see.

With barely much use left, why not trade it to me?"

His fingers ran through themselves meticulously,

Grinning, uncontrollably, he thought I was sold.

"What's in it for me?" I asked.

"Perceptive, aren't we? How about I quench that thirst?

Satiate your hunger.

No woe will grip you anymore!" he exclaimed.

A gust of wind blew through,

A flap of his jacket revealed the hole in his chest.

He smiled.

"Surely you know," he said, "another's heart cannot fill

someone else's hole."

"Then what do you need it for?" I snapped.

"This suffering has been dreadful,

But I carry on nonetheless.

What's your motive?"

"Oh, come now," he backtracked. "I simply enjoy helping

others not suffer."

My heart flickered dimmer.

He looked, then turned in haste.

"Can't say I didn't warn ya,

Enjoy your last day!"

He waved, then left.

Last day?

This is already hell.

The only possible way for this to get any worse,

Is for someone else to come trying to claim they can

quench my thirst.

Acting like I have to give up hope to make it in this place

while I burn.

Then try to sell it to me in the process?

Absolutely absurd.

What's next,

They try to take it from me?

I tread on,

So tired,

But what is tired in a place with no time?

I begin to fall over in a daze.

A demon quick as light snatches my heart.

He passed by me,

So tired, I'm not even phased.

"Sucker!"

He bolted off in the distance.

I'm stuck now with one knee on the ground.

I look down, and feel my heart still flicker.

It may not be there, but I know I still got it.
I stand up, shatter the ground in an instant.
A fissure.
Split the air as I followed him.
The quickest persistence.
I followed that demon for ages,
Chased him through mazes.
Patience.
Till finally he stopped at a gate.
So massive, it slowly opened.
I crept in behind him, unnoticed, and watched closely.
He entered a great hall with a throne that had a presence.
He kneeled before it and held my heart up with two
hands.
"I have brought you another, my lord" he cried out.
"Will you please give me some hope?"
The throne with a presence was heavy and dark.
A giant old man looked down and picked up my heart.
It flickered, less bright than ever.
The old man laughed so loud that my throat became dry
again.
"You have brought me a dud, mere nothingness to me.
But you did well, so I will give you a gift."
The old man placed a dark heart in the demon's chest.
The demon's eyes went blank, and he slowly walked away.
The old man looked over to see me hiding,
Before I knew it, I was standing in front of him.
Blank face on me, inside a sea that is writhing.

"Here," he tossed the heart to me.

"You better get going."

I caught the heart and looked up in confusion.

"What did you do to him?" I asked.

"Why was he in that trance?"

The old man sighed and leaned forward with comfort.

"False hope brings peace to those that quit.

I merely give the people of this realm the ability to
reprieve their suffering.

Everything has a consequence, though,

And they will wander aimlessly with no real hope."

"Are they happy?" I asked.

He grins with acceptance.

"Who knows?" he said. "If they chose it themselves, then
that's all that counts.

That little heart you got there won't leave you, though,

Crumble,

Or die out.

Can't really say you belong here.

Are you on vacation? Or just lost?"

I looked down.

Ashamed.

"I'm not sure. I just feel like I've been here for too long and
that's all I know."

I looked up.

The old man's face and presence was not as heavy or intim-
idating as it was before.

He sat back and scratched his beard.

"Hmmmmm…. Could've been close to losing hope.
But maybe your heart realized that was a fake freedom all
along."
He snapped his fingers, and his face lit up.
"I got it!
How about I send you back to where that heart is from?"
My heart grew brighter and hummed a soft tune.
As I smiled, I said, "I would love that.
I promise if I come back, I'll visit again."
He laughed.
Though this time, I laughed too, and my throat wasn't dry.
"You said it, not me, but I won't count on it."
He winked and snapped.
I awoke to the light.
Something fresh.
Smells like green.
Smells like life.
I look down, there's no heart,
Just a pencil in my hand,
I'm back at it again.